CONTEMPORARY'S

PRE-GED

LITERATURE AND
THE ARTS

CONTEMPORARY BOOKS

a division of NTC/Contemporary Publishing Group
Lincolnwood, Illinois USA

Project Editor
Cathy Niemet

Series Developer
The Wheetley Company. Inc.

ISBN: 0-8092-3491-2

Published by Contemporary Books,
a division of NTC/Contemporary Publishing Group, Inc.,
4255 West Touhy Avenue,
Lincolnwood (Chicago), Illinois 60646-1975 U.S.A.
© 1995 by NTC/Contemporary Publishing Group, Inc.
Manufactured in the United States of America.

9 0 GB(H)) 10 9 8 7 6 5

Editorial Director
Mark Boone

Editorial
Nancy Parsegian
Sandra Hazel
Joyce Goldenstern
Lisa Black

Editorial Production Manager
Norma Underwood

Production Editor/
Electronic Composition
Thomas D. Scharf

Cover Design
Michael Kelly

Interior Design
Lucy Lesiak

Illustrations
The Wheetley Company, Inc.

Contents

Acknowledgments

Excerpt on page 2 from *USA Today*, copyright © 1984. Reprinted with permission.

Excerpt on page 3 from *2010: Odyssey Two* by Arthur C. Clarke. Copyright © 1982 by Serebdib BV. Reprinted by permission of Ballantine Books, a division of Random House, Inc.

Poem on page 4 "Richard Cory" from *Children of the Night* by Edwin Arlington Robinson. Copyright © 1897, Charles Scribner's Sons, Inc. Reprinted by permission.

Review on page 5 of *Black Beauty* by Johanna Steinmetz, the *Chicago Tribune*, July 29, 1994. Reprinted by permission of the author.

Adaptation on page 6 from *Your Silent Language* by Elizabeth McGough, Copyright © 1974 by Elizabeth McGough. Reprinted by permission of Morrow Junior Books, a division of William Morrow & Company, Inc.

Excerpt on page 7 from "The Season of Divorce" in *The Stories of John Cheever*. Copyright © 1950 and renewed 1978 by John Cheever. Reprinted by permission of Alfred A. Knopf, Inc.

Excerpt on page 8 from *A Raisin in the Sun* by Lorraine Hansberry. Copyright © 1959, 1966, 1984 by Robert Nemiroff. Reprinted by permission of Random House, Inc.

Excerpt on page 35 from *The Skylark of Space* by E. E. Smith. Copyright © 1946, 1947 by E. E. Smith, renewed 1974 by the estate of E. E. Smith. Reprinted by permission of James Allen, Literary Agent.

Excerpt on page 41 from *Reader's Digest*, April 1982. Reprinted with permission of *Reader's Digest*.

Excerpt on page 43 from *The World Book Encyclopedia*. Copyright © 1955, World Book, Inc. Reprinted by permission of the publisher.

Excerpt on page 83 is from *The Medium is the Message* by Marshall McLuhan and Quentin Fiore. Copyright © Jerome Agel. Published by Touchstone Books/Simon & Schuster, Inc. Reprinted with permission of Jerome Agel.

Excerpt on page 84 from "Mining Part of Early History" in *Uplands,* published by the *Dodgeville Chronicle*. Reprinted by permission of the publisher.

Excerpt on page 93 from *Chesapeake* by James A. Michener. Copyright © 1978 by Random House, Inc. Reprinted by permission of the publisher.

Story "Early Autumn" on pages 94–95 from *Something in Common* by Langston Hughes. Copyright © 1963 by Langston Hughes, renewed 1991 by Arnold Rampersad and Ramona Bass. Reprinted by permission of Hill and Wang, a division of Farrar, Straus & Giroux, Inc.

Excerpt on page 100 from *Airport* by Arthur Hailey. Copyright © 1968 by Arthur Hailey. Reprinted by permission of Doubleday, a division of Bantam Doubleday Dell Publishing Group, Inc.

Excerpt on page 102 from "A Worn Path" by Eudora Welty in *A Curtain of Green and Other Stories*. Copyright © 1941, 1969 by Eudora Welty. Reprinted by permission of Harcourt Brace & Company.

Excerpt on page 104 from *The Old Man and the Sea* by Ernest Hemingway. Copyright © 1952 by Ernest Hemingway, renewed 1980 by Mary Hemingway. Reprinted by permission of Scribner, an imprint of Simon & Schuster, Inc.

Excerpt on page 110 from *The Grapes of Wrath* by John Steinbeck. Copyright © 1939, renewed 1967 by John Steinbeck. Reprinted by permission of Viking Penguin, a division of Penguin Books USA, Inc.

Excerpt on page 112 from *Holy the Firm* by Annie Dillard. Copyright © 1977 by Annie Dillard. Reprinted by permission of HarperCollins Publishers, Inc.

Excerpt on page 117 from "Census" in *Simple's Uncle Sam* by Langston Hughes. Copyright © 1965 by Langston Hughes, renewed 1993 by Arnold Rampersad and Ramona Bass. Reprinted by permission of Hill and Wang, a division of Farrar, Straus & Giroux, Inc.

Excerpt on page 118 from *Ordinary People* by Judith Guest. Copyright © 1976 by Judith Guest. Reprinted by permission of Viking Penguin, a division of Penguin Books USA, Inc.

Excerpt on page 119 from *Catch-22* by Joseph Heller. Copyright © 1955, 1961 by Joseph Heller, renewed 1989. Reprinted by permission of Simon & Schuster, Inc.

Poem on page 123 "A Sad Song About Greenwich Village" by Frances Park. Copyright © 1927, 1955 by Frances Park. Reprinted by permission of The New Yorker Magazine, Inc.

To the Student

Congratulations on your decision to use *Pre-GED Literature and the Arts* to strengthen your critical-thinking skills in the areas of literal understanding, making inferences, and analyzing literature and the arts ideas. You will also learn how to read nonfiction prose, prose fiction, poetry, drama, and commentaries on the arts selections.

Here is an overview of what you will find in this book, along with some tips on using the book.

Literature and the Arts Pre-Test   The Pre-Test, found on pages 1–13, will help you decide which skills you need to work on the most. It will direct you to the parts of the book you may want to spend the most time with.

Chapter 1: Literal Understanding   By working through Chapter 1, you will review how to find the main idea of a paragraph and of a passage, how to identify the purpose of a selection and its supporting details, and how to use context clues to unlock the meaning of unknown words.

Chapter 2: Making Inferences   In this chapter you will learn how to make inferences, draw conclusions, and apply what you've learned from one situation to another.

Chapter 3: Analyzing Literature and the Arts Ideas   This chapter teaches you how to recognize the patterns in which materials are presented, such as order of importance, sequence of events, cause and effect, comparison and contrast, and classification. You will also learn how to analyze style and tone.

Chapter 4: Nonfiction Prose   In this chapter you will learn how to read nonfiction prose, recognize the difference between fact and opinion, detect an author's bias, and read and interpret material from newspapers, periodicals, and editorials.

Chapter 5: Prose Fiction   This chapter introduces you to the elements of fiction: setting, plot, character, and point of view. You will also learn how to interpret literal and figurative language and the theme of a short story.

Chapter 6: Poetry   In this chapter you will learn what poetry is and how to read it. You will also learn to infer a poem's meaning and understand how the use of imagery and figurative language contribute to a poem's effect.

Chapter 7: Drama   This chapter introduces you to the elements of drama. You will learn how to interpret stage directions, punctuation, and how to read dialogue. You will also discover how character and action are important to drama.

Chapter 8: Commentaries on the Arts   In this chapter you will read reviews, essays, and commentaries about radio and television, the performing and visual arts, and literature. As you interpret commentaries, you will learn how to distinguish between fact and opinion and analyze the descriptive language used.

Writing Activities   Every chapter allows you an opportunity to practice different types of writing and, in this way, improve your writing skills.

Pre-GED Practice   At the end of every chapter, and sometimes more frequently throughout the book, you will find one or more passages that are formatted with five-item multiple-choice questions to help you prepare for GED-level study. The Pre-GED Practice at the end of each chapter serves as a review of the skills you have learned in the chapter.

Literature and the Arts Post-Test   The Post-Test, found on pages 185–199, will help you to see how well you have learned the critical-thinking and reading skills presented in this book. The Post-Test consists of 40 multiple-choice questions.

Answer Key   This feature gives answers and explanations for all the questions in this book. Use the Answer Key only after you have attempted to answer a set of questions in an exercise.

Glossary   Throughout the book, key terms that are important for you to know are printed in boldface and italic type and are defined in the glossary at the back of the book.

Pre-Test

The Literature and the Arts Pre-Test that follows is a guide to using this book. Take the Pre-Test before you begin working on any of the chapters. The test consists of 30 multiple-choice questions that test the reading and reasoning skills in literature and the arts covered in this book. All of the questions are based on fiction and nonfiction prose, poetry, drama, and commentaries on the arts.

Answer each question as carefully as possible. Choose the best of five answer choices by filling in the corresponding circle on the answer grid. If a question is too difficult, go ahead and come back to that question later. When you have completed the test, check your answers on page 11.

Using the Evaluation Chart on page 13, circle the number of each question that you missed. If you missed many of the questions that correspond to a certain reading skill, you will want to pay special attention to that skill as you work your way through this book.

1 ① ② ③ ④ ⑤	9 ① ② ③ ④ ⑤	17 ① ② ③ ④ ⑤	25 ① ② ③ ④ ⑤
2 ① ② ③ ④ ⑤	10 ① ② ③ ④ ⑤	18 ① ② ③ ④ ⑤	26 ① ② ③ ④ ⑤
3 ① ② ③ ④ ⑤	11 ① ② ③ ④ ⑤	19 ① ② ③ ④ ⑤	27 ① ② ③ ④ ⑤
4 ① ② ③ ④ ⑤	12 ① ② ③ ④ ⑤	20 ① ② ③ ④ ⑤	28 ① ② ③ ④ ⑤
5 ① ② ③ ④ ⑤	13 ① ② ③ ④ ⑤	21 ① ② ③ ④ ⑤	29 ① ② ③ ④ ⑤
6 ① ② ③ ④ ⑤	14 ① ② ③ ④ ⑤	22 ① ② ③ ④ ⑤	30 ① ② ③ ④ ⑤
7 ① ② ③ ④ ⑤	15 ① ② ③ ④ ⑤	23 ① ② ③ ④ ⑤	
8 ① ② ③ ④ ⑤	16 ① ② ③ ④ ⑤	24 ① ② ③ ④ ⑤	

Questions 1–4 refer to the following newspaper article.

Hispanics to Undertake Citizenship Campaign

Hispanics are mounting a nationwide drive to get Hispanic immigrants to become U.S. citizens. About 5.91 million Hispanic adults in the
5 USA aren't citizens—partly because of their fear of dealing with immigration officials.

They can't vote, serve on juries, work for the government, or qualify for
10 some federal education benefits, said Harry Pachon, head of the National Association of Latino Elected and Appointed Officials (NALEAO).

Saturday, NALEAO will sponsor a
15 conference in Washington, D.C. On the agenda: a proposal to create task forces for a nationwide citizenship drive for Hispanics—the USA's second-largest minority, projected to be the
20 biggest by the year 2020. Hispanics' naturalization rate is 30 percent, compared to 44 percent for non-Hispanics, says an NALEAO study.

"Citizenship used to be a highly
25 esteemed value in the 1920s and 1930s," Pachon said. "We're hoping to revive that." The problem is most acute among Mexicans—who make up 64 percent of all Hispanics. Mariana
30 Scuros of the Mexican American Legal Defense and Education Fund said many Mexicans—with a naturalization rate of only 16 percent—don't seek citizenship because they misunderstand
35 it. "They think they have to step on the Mexican flag," said Scuros. "The Mexican is very proud of his heritage."

—Excerpted from *USA Today,* 1984

1. What is the naturalization rate of Mexicans in the United States?
   - **(1)** 5.91 million
   - **(2)** 30 percent
   - **(3)** 44 percent
   - **(4)** 16 percent
   - **(5)** 64 percent

2. Why do many Hispanics choose not to seek U.S. citizenship?
   - **(1)** As illegal immigrants, they are afraid of being turned down.
   - **(2)** They have no wish to vote or serve on juries.
   - **(3)** They fear dealing with immigration officials.
   - **(4)** They don't know how to go about applying for citizenship.
   - **(5)** They are planning to leave the United States.

3. The goal of the NALEAO conference is to
   - **(1)** encourage Hispanics to register to vote
   - **(2)** mount a national citizenship drive for Hispanics
   - **(3)** raise the Hispanic naturalization rate from 30 to 44 percent
   - **(4)** make Hispanics the largest U.S. minority group by the year 2020
   - **(5)** help Hispanics who want to immigrate to the United States

4. Which of the following does the article imply is an advantage of U.S. citizenship?
   - **(1)** eligibility for federal education assistance
   - **(2)** better wages
   - **(3)** the opportunity to work in the United States
   - **(4)** membership in what is fast becoming the largest U.S. minority
   - **(5)** separation from one's native country

Questions 5–8 refer to the following passage.

"You're not scared, are you?" asked Max, when they were about to put on their helmets.

"Not enough to make a mess in my
5   suit. Otherwise, yes."

Max chuckled. "I'd say that's about right for this job. But don't worry—I'll get you there in one piece, with my— what do you call it?"

10   "Broomstick. Because witches are supposed to ride them."

"Oh, yes. Have you ever used one?"

"I tried once, but mine got away
15   from me. Everyone else thought it was very funny."

There are some professions which have evolved unique and characteristic tools—the longshoreman's hook, the
20   potter's wheel, the bricklayer's trowel, the geologist's hammer. The men who had to spend much of their time on zero-gravity construction projects had developed the broomstick.

25   It was very simple—a hollow tube just a meter long, with a footpad at one end and a retaining loop at the other. At the touch of a button, it could telescope out to five or six times its normal length,
30   and the internal shock-absorbing system allowed a skilled operator to perform the most amazing maneuvers [movements]. The footpad could also become a claw or hook if necessary;
35   there were many other refinements, but that was the basic design. It looked deceptively easy to use; it wasn't.

The airlock pumps finished recycling; the EXIT sign came on; the
40   outer doors opened, and they drifted slowly into the void.

Discovery was windmilling about two hundred meters away, following them in orbit around *Io,* which filled half
45   the sky. Jupiter was invisible, on the other side of the satellite.

—Excerpted from *2010: Odyssey Two,* by Arthur C. Clarke

5. You can infer that the character lost his broomstick (lines 14–15) because

(1) he was overconfident
(2) he was using a difficult instrument
(3) the broomstick fell out of his hands
(4) he used it in zero gravity
(5) the internal shock absorbers failed

6. The passage suggests that *Io* seemed to be

(1) smaller than Jupiter
(2) far from Jupiter
(3) the same size as Jupiter
(4) a shield above Jupiter
(5) larger than Jupiter

7. What is the meaning of the word *telescope* (line 28)?

(1) focus
(2) magnify
(3) lash
(4) stretch
(5) drift

8. You can conclude that Max and his companion

(1) are on a geological excursion
(2) have invented an amazing new method of transportation
(3) are astronomers observing planets through a telescope
(4) are using a device like a broomstick to travel through space
(5) are trying to return to Earth from an alien planet

Questions 9–13 refer to the following poem.

Richard Cory

Whenever Richard Cory went down town,
We people on the pavement looked at him:
He was a gentleman from sole to crown,
Clean favored, and imperially slim.

5 And he was always quietly arrayed,
And he was always human when he talked;
But still he fluttered pulses when he said,
"Good-morning," and he glittered when he walked.

And he was rich—yes, richer than a king—
10 And admirably schooled in every grace:
In fine, we thought that he was everything
To make us wish that we were in his place.

So on we worked, and waited for the light,
And went without the meat, and cursed the bread;
15 And Richard Cory, one calm summer night,
Went home and put a bullet through his head.

—Edwin Arlington Robinson

9. The phrase "he glittered when he walked" (line 8) means that Richard Cory

(1) wore shiny clothing with sequins
(2) had an unusual way of walking
(3) impressed people with his elegance and wealth
(4) glared angrily at anyone who looked at him
(5) was cruel by nature

10. Which of the following best summarizes the poet's message?

(1) Richard Cory was the nicest man in town.
(2) The love of money is the root of all evil.
(3) Rich men can be as friendly as poor men.
(4) Men with money are not always content with their lives.
(5) Poor men are happier than wealthy men.

11. What happens at the end of this poem?

(1) The people clamor for the execution of Richard Cory.
(2) Richard Cory gives his wealth to charity.
(3) One of the poor townspeople kills Richard Cory.
(4) Richard Cory dies of old age.
(5) Richard Cory commits suicide.

12. "He was a gentleman from sole to crown" (line 3) means that Richard Cory

(1) was a king
(2) was not the gentleman he appeared to be
(3) wore expensive, hand-made hats and shoes
(4) was truly a gentleman
(5) cared only about his physical appearance

13. If you were one of the "people on the pavement," how would you have viewed Richard Cory?

(1) with suspicion
(2) with anger
(3) with envy
(4) with worry
(5) coldly

Questions 14 and 15 refer to the following passage.

There is no more benign [gentle and harmless] film likely to be released this summer—this year, for that matter—than *Black Beauty*, an
5   adaptation of Anna Sewell's 1877 novel about the life of a horse.

The novel, which takes place in the days when horses were valued more for work than for beauty and raised English
10 consciousness regarding their treatment, is narrated by the horse itself. The movie follows suit.

This takes a little getting used to, since talking horses generally confine
15 themselves to animation and rarely take themselves seriously even then. But Black Beauty is nothing if not earnest. It's part of his charm.

"Sold?" he cries at one point (in the
20 voice of Alan Cumming). "Every horse knows that terrifying word." Later in the story, having spotted his onetime sweetheart, Ginger, he sighs, "That night I dreamed of her, of what was and
25 of what might have been."

Black Beauty is solid craftsmanship but not flashy moviemaking. It's pretty and a trifle bland, but engaging enough to entertain
30 a wide range of ages. Best of all, it does so without trauma and without distorting the story's general message of kindness to conform to some of today's political agendas regarding animals.

—Excerpted from a movie review by Johanna Steinmetz, *Chicago Tribune*, July 29, 1994

14. This review is of a movie adapted from a(n)

(1) earlier movie
(2) English novel narrated by Alan Cumming
(3) Anna Sewell novel that is narrated by a horse
(4) benign animation
(5) political agenda

15. This review says the movie's good points include all of the following EXCEPT

(1) solid craftsmanship
(2) the earnest charm of the horse
(3) suitability for audiences of all ages
(4) blandness
(5) a simple message of kindness toward animals

Questions 16–18 refer to the following passage.

Researchers say that couples who have had a quarrel are often quite formal toward each other at a party. They touch very little, or if one reaches
5   out, the other responds by withdrawing the hand or arm touched. Dr. Edward Hall has written in *Hidden Dimension* that "the hardened, armorlike resistance to the unwanted touch . . . is a message
10 of one body to another that has universal meaning."

Have you ever seen a girl "hanging all over her boyfriend"? Nancy, who has just begun dating, feels compelled to
15 hang on Bill's arm or to have her arm around him all the time. Bill is considered a prize catch, and Nancy is proud to be seen with him. She signals ownership, as well as the need for
20 security. This behavior can be stifling.

Dr. Haim Ginott, in *Between Parent and Teenager*, told this story: Jean walked along the beach with her mother. She asked, "Mom, how do you
25 hold a husband after you've finally gotten him?"

Her mother gave her a silent lesson in love. She scooped up two handfuls of sand. One she squeezed
30 hard. The more she squeezed, the more sand escaped. The other she held lightly, and the sand remained.

Jean said, "I see."

Our society has placed taboos on
35 touch. We often equate physical contact with sex, even though in some situations a sexual message is clearly not intended. Perhaps this attitude explains why we use touching so
40 sparingly to show warmth and affection.

—Adapted from *Your Silent Language*, by Elizabeth McGough

16. What is the best title for this passage?
    (1) Mother Knows Best
    (2) Dating Dos and Don'ts
    (3) Our Greatest Fear
    (4) The Meanings of Touch
    (5) Saving Your Marriage

17. The story from Dr. Haim Ginott illustrates
    (1) the dangers of love
    (2) the difference between possessiveness and love
    (3) a scientific principle
    (4) the many meanings of love
    (5) a bitter lesson about love

18. What assumption can you make about a couple who treat each other very formally?
    (1) They want reassurance.
    (2) One of them is trying too hard to hang on to the other.
    (3) Their behavior is stifling.
    (4) They are proud to be seen together.
    (5) They have recently quarreled.

Questions 19–22 refer to the following passage.

"He stares at me," she said. "He sighs and stares at me." I know what my wife looks like in the playground. She wears an old tweed coat,
5 overshoes, and Army gloves, and a scarf is tied under her chin. The playground is a fenced and paved lot between a slum and the river. The picture of the well-dressed, pink-
10 cheeked doctor losing his heart to Ethel in this environment was hard to take seriously. She didn't mention him then for several days, and I guessed that he had stopped his visits. Ethel's birthday
15 came at the end of the month, and I forgot about it, but when I came home that evening, there were a lot of roses in the living room. They were a birthday present from Trencher, she told me. I
20 was cross at myself for having forgotten her birthday, and Trencher's roses made me angry. I asked her if she'd seen him recently.

"Oh, yes," she said, "he still comes
25 to the playground nearly every afternoon. I haven't told you, have I? He's made his declaration. He loves me. He can't live without me. He'd walk through fire to hear the notes of my
30 voice." She laughed. "That's what he said."

"When did he say this?"

"At the playground. And walking home. Yesterday."

35 "How long has he known?"

"That's the funny part about it," she said. "He knew before he met me at the Newsomes' that night. He saw me waiting for a crosstown bus about three
40 weeks before that. He just saw me and he said that he knew then, the minute he saw me. Of course, he's crazy."

—Excerpted from "*The Season of Divorce*," by John Cheever

19. The main subject of this passage is
(1) Ethel's behavior at the playground
(2) a developing relationship between Ethel and Trencher
(3) an argument between Ethel and her husband
(4) Ethel's birthday
(5) the narrator's lack of interest in his wife's affairs

20. What is Trencher's occupation?
(1) playground supervisor
(2) bus driver
(3) salesman
(4) florist
(5) doctor

21. Trencher's declaration that "he'd walk through fire" to hear Ethel's voice means that he
(1) loves music
(2) has lost touch with reality
(3) would do anything to be with Ethel
(4) is attracted to fire
(5) can't resist the sound of Ethel's voice

22. Which of the following best describes the narrator's feelings about Trencher's odd relationship with Ethel?
(1) He takes no interest at first but becomes annoyed when Trencher sends roses.
(2) He is angry at his wife for paying attention to Trencher.
(3) His early annoyance gives way to a feeling of happiness for his wife.
(4) He thinks the whole thing is very funny.
(5) He is upset that Ethel is making up lies about Trencher.

Questions 23–26 refer to the following excerpt from a play.

WALTER: I want so many things that they are driving me kind of crazy, . . . Mama—look at me.

MAMA: I'm looking at you. You a good-looking boy. You got a job, a nice wife, a fine boy and—

WALTER: A job. [*Looks at her*] Mama, a job? I open and close car doors all day long. I drive a man around in his limousine and I say, "Yes, sir; no, sir; very good, sir; shall I take the Drive, sir?" Mama, that ain't no kind of job . . . that ain't nothing at all. [*Very quietly*] Mama, I don't know if I can make you understand.

MAMA: Understand what, baby?

WALTER: [*Quietly*] Sometimes it's like I can see the future stretched out in front of me—just plain as day. The future, Mama. Hanging over there at the edge of my days. Just waiting for me—a big, looming blank space—full of nothing. Just waiting for me. [*Pause*]

Sometimes when I'm downtown and I pass them cool, quiet-looking restaurants where them white boys are sitting back and talking 'bout things . . . sitting there turning deals worth millions of dollars . . . sometimes I see guys don't look much older than me—

MAMA: Son—how come you talk so much 'bout money?

WALTER: [*With immense passion*] Because it is life.

MAMA: [*Quietly*] Oh—[*Very quietly*] So now it is life. Money is life. Once upon a time freedom used to be life—now it's money. I guess the world really do change.

WALTER: No—it was always money, Mama. We just didn't know about it.

MAMA: No . . . something has changed. [*She looks at him*] You something new, boy. In my time we was worried about not being lynched and getting to the North if we could and how to stay alive and still have a pinch of dignity too. . . . Now here come you and Beneatha—talking 'bout things we ain't never even thought about hardly, me and your daddy. You ain't satisfied or proud of nothing we done. I mean that you had a home; that we kept you out of trouble till you was grown; that you don't have to ride to work on the back of nobody's streetcar—You my children—but how different we done become.

WALTER: You just don't understand, Mama, you just don't understand.

—Excerpted from *A Raisin in the Sun,* by Lorraine Hansberry

23. Which of the following is most important to Walter?

- **(1)** a secure job
- **(2)** an understanding mother
- **(3)** a loving wife
- **(4)** money
- **(5)** his son

24. In Mama's opinion, Walter

- **(1)** thinks too much about money
- **(2)** has a degrading job
- **(3)** takes his wife and son for granted
- **(4)** is too young to worry about the future
- **(5)** should be more helpful to her

25. Mama's attitude toward Walter is one of

- **(1)** anger
- **(2)** disappointment
- **(3)** indifference
- **(4)** understanding
- **(5)** nurturing

26. What is Walter's occupation?

- **(1)** taxi driver
- **(2)** clerk
- **(3)** chauffeur
- **(4)** waiter
- **(5)** bus driver

Questions 27–30 refer to the following passage.

I was at first very uncomfortable in that strange country. Although I could handle the language well, I seemed to be making a lot of mistakes somehow. It
5   was obvious that people were beginning to think I was very cold, even though I felt very friendly toward them. Slowly it began to dawn on me that my sense of distance was different from theirs.

10   I saw a man I barely knew approaching me on a road one day. He began to wave when he was still forty feet from me and was talking when he was yet twenty feet away. I did not
15   respond at all until he was within ten feet of me: I waved. I began my hellos when we were about five feet apart. I hadn't even realized that he had been waving at me from that great distance. I
20   didn't know that he had been talking to me from twenty feet away. By the time I responded to seeing him, he had already begun to think I had insulted him.

25   Another time, when I was being introduced to someone, I extended my hand to shake his. He held my hand so long that I began to feel uncomfortable and finally had to pull away. The
30   conversation didn't last long. The man thought me impolite. My own background had taught me that a handshake should last about two seconds; his culture prescribed a
35   handshake of nearly a half-minute with the last twenty seconds more like holding hands than a handshake.

Once I learned to begin waving from farther away and to hold a
40   handshake for thirty seconds, people stopped regarding me as cold. But I had

to change the sense of distance I had grown up with. I had to understand that forty feet was close enough to wave and
45 that holding hands with a stranger was nothing more than basic courtesy.

27. What does this passage compare?

(1) an American and someone from another country

(2) waving and shaking hands

(3) two cultures

(4) politeness and rudeness

(5) language and behavior

28. How long did a polite handshake last in the "strange country"?

(1) two seconds

(2) twenty seconds

(3) one minute

(4) half a minute

(5) a minute and a half

29. The author became accustomed to waving from farther away and holding hands for a longer time because

(1) he disliked his own culture

(2) he did not want to offend anyone

(3) he was tired of being bothered by strangers

(4) it was required by law

(5) he enjoyed change

30. At first, the author was most comfortable with

(1) the sense of distance

(2) the language

(3) changes in his diet

(4) the new customs

(5) the behavior of strangers

ANSWERS ARE ON PAGE 11.

Pre-Test Answer Key

1. **(4)** This information is stated in the last paragraph.
2. **(3)** This information appears in the first paragraph.
3. **(2)** The third paragraph states that "a proposal to create task forces for a nationwide citizenship drive" was on the agenda.
4. **(1)** The article states that some federal educational benefits are not available to noncitizens.
5. **(2)** The passage states that the character had "tried it once" and that the broomstick looked "deceptively easy to use."
6. **(5)** Since Io "filled half the sky" and Jupiter "was invisible," you can infer that Io appeared larger.
7. **(4)** The passage says the broomstick could "telescope out to five or six times its normal length." *Stretch* is the best possible choice.
8. **(4)** Lines 38–41 mention a departure. From this and the discussions of the broomstick and zero gravity, you can infer that they are traveling in space.
9. **(3)** This is figurative language. It refers to Richard Cory's wealth and elegance.
10. **(4)** See the third stanza. The people wished they could be in Richard Cory's place. They did not know how unhappy he was.
11. **(5)** The poem states that he "put a bullet through his head."
12. **(4)** "From sole to crown" is figurative language meaning totally or completely. *Was truly a gentleman* is the best possible choice.
13. **(3)** The last line in the third stanza says the townspeople wished they could change places with Richard Cory. *Envy* best describes this sentiment.
14. **(3)** The first paragraph says that the movie is based on the novel by Anna Sewell. The second explains that the novel's narrator is a horse.

15. **(4)** Blandness (which means dullness) is not a compliment. All of the other points are specifically made in the review.
16. **(4)** The theme of the whole passage is how touching and purposeful separation indicate certain feelings.
17. **(2)** Dr. Ginott uses the analogy of the sand in the hand to teach that by holding something too tightly, one risks losing it.
18. **(5)** The key research findings are presented in the first paragraph. Following an argument, couples tend to treat each other with cold formality.
19. **(2)** Most of the description and all of the conversation deal with the developing relationship between Ethel and Trencher.
20. **(5)** The author refers to this in line 10
21. **(3)** This is an example of figurative (nonliteral) language. It means that Trencher is so taken with Ethel he would do anything just to see her.
22. **(1)** Until Trencher sent the roses, the narrator found this relationship "hard to take seriously." But once he saw the flowers, he began asking questions.
23. **(4)** In lines 41–42 Walter tells his mother that "money is life."
24. **(1)** Throughout the passage, to his mother's dismay, Walter stresses the importance of money.
25. **(2)** Mama quietly expresses disappointment in her son's outlook.
26. **(3)** This can be inferred from lines 9–14.
27. **(3)** This passage emphasizes the differences between the cultures of the author's native land and the country he visits.
28. **(4)** This is stated in lines 34–35.
29. **(2)** The author mentions that before he changed his ways, people he met thought he was cold and impolite. He changed his behavior to correct this situation.
30. **(2)** Lines 2–3 mention the author's ease with the language.

Use the answer key on page 11 to check your answers to the Pre-Test. Then, on the chart below, circle the numbers of the questions you missed. Note the areas where you missed more than half of the questions. The reading skills on pages 17–65 are very important for success in GED-level study.

Skill Area/ Content Area	Literal Comprehension	Inferential Comprehension	Analysis	Application
Nonfiction Prose (pages 69–87)	1, 2, 28, 30	3, 17, 27	4, 16, 29	18
Prose Fiction (pages 89–119)	20	5, 7, 21, 22	6, 8, 19	
Poetry (pages 121–139)	11	12	9, 10	13
Drama (pages 141–153)	26	24	23, 25	
Commentaries on the Arts (pages 155–183)	14		15	

CRITICAL THINKING SKILLS IN LITERATURE AND THE ARTS

■ Literal Understanding
■ Making Inferences
■ Analyzing Literature and the Arts Ideas

1 Literal Understanding

In this chapter, you will study three basic reading skills: main ideas, supporting details, and context clues.

Each section of this chapter teaches a particular skill through explanations and practice exercises. Read the introductory material first. Then read the selections and do the exercises. Use the Answer Key to check your answers. Be sure to study the explanations of any questions you missed.

The ***main idea*** is a statement that tells what the whole selection is about. When a passage consists of only one paragraph, the main idea is the same for both passage and paragraph. In longer passages, each paragraph has its own main idea, and so does the passage as a whole.

To find the main idea of a passage, you must first learn how to find the main idea of a paragraph.

THE MAIN IDEA OF A PARAGRAPH

Every paragraph should have a main idea. The main idea tells what the whole paragraph is about. To find the main idea of a paragraph, follow these steps:

1. Read the entire paragraph.

2. Decide what the paragraph is saying. What is it about?

3. Reread the first and last sentences. The main idea of a paragraph is usually expressed first or last.

Directions: Read the paragraph below. Put a check in front of the main idea of the paragraph.

Television feeds us a constant diet of violence and sex. When we wake up, the morning news greets us with the latest mass murders, earthquakes, and plane crashes. On game shows, the hosts and contestants trade sexy words and gestures as they smooch their way to the big prize. Soap operas serve up a menu of adultery, abortion, and agony. The evening news replays the morning news, in case we forget. The final fare of the day is nighttime television. Here we may gorge on a cops-and-robbers shoot-out or nibble on a shallow tale of lust on the ranch.

_____

_____

The main idea of this paragraph is that

_____ **(1)** television programs are not fit for young children because of the violence and sex

_____ **(2)** some of the sex and violence on television centers around disasters, adultery, and crime

_____ **(3)** game shows and soap operas promote sex more than violence

_____ **(4)** from morning to night, television programs deluge viewers with violence and sex

The main idea is best stated in choice (4). It is also expressed in the first sentence of the paragraph. The rest of the paragraph develops this idea with details of the excessive violence and sex on television.

Look at the other choices. You may have read or heard the idea in choice (1) elsewhere, but it is not stated in this paragraph. Although choice (2) is mentioned in the paragraph, it does not convey what the whole paragraph is about. The paragraph doesn't make the comparison mentioned in choice (3).

The main idea of a paragraph is often, but not always, in the first sentence. For example, we could easily move the first sentence in our television paragraph. Try it. Cross it out and rewrite it on the blank lines at the end. Now we have a paragraph whose main idea is in the last sentence. All the other sentences give supporting details.

To find the main idea of a paragraph, then, begin by looking at the first sentence. If you don't find it there, try the last sentence. In some cases, the main idea is in the middle of the paragraph. How can you recognize it? It will express what the whole paragraph is about.

THE MAIN IDEA OF A PASSAGE

You know that a passage consists of one or more related paragraphs. You have also learned that a passage, like a paragraph, should have a main idea.

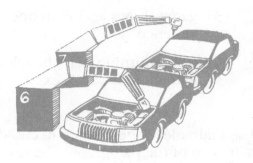

Today, people are changing careers frequently. Ten to twenty years ago, such a concept was unheard of. People usually looked forward to working at the same job for their entire lives. Now people of all ages often think about and make career changes. In fact, job counselors
5   estimate that, in tomorrow's marketplace, workers will change careers three or four times during their lives.

Right now, thousands of laid-off steel and auto workers wait for callbacks to jobs that have been eliminated. Even newer fields, such as computer programming, are becoming completely filled. As unemploy-
10   ment hovers around 10 percent, we find people entering new job fields out of necessity. Thus, today's uncertain economy contributes to the rapid changes in the job market.

Additionally, new fields, such as robotics, have recently emerged on the scene. Instead of people, lifelike robots now assemble everything
15   from cars and clocks to appliances and packaged foods. Also, people now produce tiny computers that control wristwatches, heart monitors, and nuclear warheads. In such ways, technology accelerates, or speeds up, the rate of change in the marketplace.

The preceding passage consists of three paragraphs. For each paragraph underline the one sentence that best expresses the main idea.

Did you find the main ideas of each paragraph?

The main idea of the first paragraph is given in the first sentence. Career changes are becoming increasingly common. The rest of the paragraph supports this idea with details.

The main idea of the second paragraph is stated in the last sentence. The economy is one factor contributing to a changing job market. The rest of the paragraph supports this idea with details about job cutbacks in various fields.

The main idea of the third paragraph also appears in the last sentence. Technology is another contributor to the changing job market. Details about robotics and computers support this idea.

Directions: Put a check in front of the statement that best expresses the main idea of the entire passage.

_____ **(1)** Society today is characterized by high unemployment, a slow economy, and new technology.

_____ **(2)** People should plan carefully to have secure jobs in the future.

_____ **(3)** Economic changes and developing technology mean frequent job changes for many workers.

You were correct if you chose statement (3) as the main idea of the entire passage.

THE PURPOSE OF A SELECTION

Look back at the paragraph about television on page 18. The main idea, as you know, is that network programming serves up a steady diet of violence and sex. But the purpose of the passage is something else. The purpose is to provide information, to inform the reader.

Some types of written material do not have main ideas, but all written material should have a purpose. Think, for a moment, about a recipe. A recipe does not have a main idea, but it certainly has a purpose. A bus schedule has no main idea either, but it, too, has a definite purpose. The general purpose of such material as directions, manuals, recipes, schedules, and advertisements is to be helpful to the reader in some specific way. In the case of advertising, the purpose is to persuade the reader to buy a particular product or service.

It is usually up to the reader to figure out the purpose of a selection. Rarely is the purpose spelled out in a single sentence. To find it, begin by reading the entire piece. Think about how you, as the reader, are supposed to use the information. Why was it written? What will be the result if you do what it says? When you can answer these questions, you have found the purpose of the material.

As you read the selection that follows, think about its purpose.

Water Heater

1. Set water heater at 140°F if you have a dishwasher, 120°F if you don't.

2. Take showers instead of baths.

3. Turn the heater down or off when you vacation.

4. If hot water isn't used all day or night, install a timer to turn the heater on when you need it, off when you don't.

The purpose of the passage is to

_____ **(1)** help readers install water-heater timers

_____ **(2)** inform readers about the temperature range of water heaters

_____ **(3)** identify the uses of a water heater

_____ **(4)** provide energy-saving tips

The purpose of the passage is choice (4), to *provide energy-saving tips*. Every sentence gives a suggestion for saving energy. The purpose is not stated in the selection. You need to figure it out for yourself.

EXERCISE 1

Directions: Read the passage below and answer the questions that follow.

For the first time in history, there are more students enrolled in colleges as part-time students than are enrolled full-time. Most of these part-time students are working people between the ages of 25 and 45; many have families.

Universities and colleges are glad to see these new, older students because they
5 bring to their campuses a kind of maturity and determination that younger students do not necessarily possess. Because of their work and family responsibilities, older students often make better, more disciplined students than do younger ones.

10   Adults are in school for various reasons. Some who already hold degrees are taking courses to broaden their knowledge in a certain area. Other adults, with degrees, return to school to prepare for career changes. Many adults return to obtain a degree. Colleges are especially interested in such students.

15   Some colleges offer life-experience credits to students. They give adults credit for work they did either as an employee or as a volunteer. Other colleges shorten the amount of time students must spend in studying the basic courses in a liberal arts program. An older adult's experience is broader than that of a younger freshman; thus, it takes less time to set up a program for study.

1. Match each paragraph listed on the left with its main idea statement on the right. Write the correct letter on the line.

_____ **Paragraph 1**   **(a)** Students attend college to get a degree, prepare for a career, or just to broaden their knowledge.

_____ **Paragraph 2**   **(b)** Colleges often adapt coursework to the needs and experiences of adults.

_____ **Paragraph 3**   **(c)** Colleges welcome older, more disciplined students.

_____ **Paragraph 4**   **(d)** Colleges now have more older part-time students than younger full-time students.

2. Put a check in front of the main idea of the passage.

_____ **(1)** There are more adult, part-time students in colleges now than ever before.

_____ **(2)** Older adults do better work in college than younger students do.

_____ **(3)** There are many opportunities for adults who wish to further their education.

_____ **(4)** Colleges are trying hard to attract older students.

3. The purpose of the passage is to

_____ **(1)** criticize

_____ **(2)** inform

_____ **(3)** evaluate

_____ **(4)** persuade

ANSWERS ARE ON PAGE 200.

SUPPORTING DETAILS

Supporting details are the facts that describe or explain the main idea of a passage. An easy way to remember the relationship between supporting details and the main idea is to picture a table. A table cannot stand without legs. Likewise, a main idea rests upon supporting information. For a thorough understanding of what you read, you must grasp both the main idea and the facts, figures, examples, and explanations that back it up, or support it.

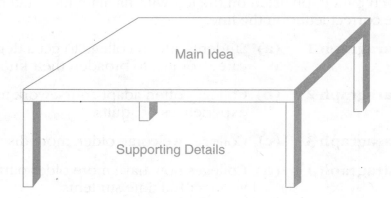

In this section, you will practice locating facts contained within passages. The technique of scanning will help you do this. You ***scan*** a passage by rereading it quickly but closely to find a specific fact or detail. As you read, concentrate only on finding the piece of information you are looking for.

To find supporting details within a selection, follow these steps:

1. Read the passage.

2. Identify the main idea.

3. Scan the passage for the specific information you need to find.

4. As you scan, remember the five Ws: *who, what, when, where,* and *why*.

EXERCISE 2

Directions: Read the following passage and then answer the questions in the space provided.

Black Hawk

Black Hawk, famous chief of the Sauk Indians, refused to leave Illinois after white men arrived in the late 1700s. When the Sauk and Fox tribes gave us their lands in 1804, he would not accept the contract. He believed that the chiefs drank firewater before signing the agreement and that the white men made the Indians drunk to trick their 5 leaders, who really did not want to give up their land.

The high point of Sauk resistance came in the Black Hawk War. In 1832, only Black Hawk's tribe remained in Illinois and Wisconsin. The other Indians had moved west to reservations. The war did not last long, and the casualties on both sides were light, but Black Hawk and his tribe were strong foes. After the Indians were defeated, Black Hawk 10 and his sons were sent with their tribe to a reservation at Fort Des Moines.

The story of Black Hawk lives on forever in his love for the land. "Keep it as we did," he said to his captors.

1. When did the Black Hawk War take place?

_____

2. Why did Black Hawk resist the white settlers?

_____

3. What did Black Hawk do?

_____

4. Who were the Sauk and the Fox?

_____

5. Where was Black Hawk sent after the war?

_____

ANSWERS ARE ON PAGE 200.

CONTEXT CLUES

When you read an unfamiliar word, you can make a good guess at its meaning from the **context**—from the way it is used and from the words around it.

If you did not know what an island was, you could probably figure it out from the context in a sentence like this:

> The *island* of Hawaii shines like a jewel, protected on all sides by the blue waters of the Pacific.

The words after *island—protected on all sides by the blue waters—* give clues to its meaning.

The following example illustrates other ways to use context clues.

> Barbara is stationed with the army in Germany. She is the *liaison* officer, or cooperating agent, for the German and American forces.

In this example, the key word *or* helps you to define *liaison*. The phrase *or cooperating agent* defines a *liaison* as "a person who helps two groups cooperate."

Other useful key words that help to define unknown words are *because, that is, means, such as*, and *is called*. Look at this example and use context clues to figure out the meaning of the *italic* word.

> *Procrastination* is called the thief of time because it always results in postponing an action.

What do you think *procrastination* means? Using the words following *is called* and *because,* you could conclude that *procrastination* is the act of postponing, or putting off, something you should do.

Another way of defining a new word is to search for its opposite meaning.

> I was *skeptical* about his promise. However, I had to believe what he said.

Note the key words in this example. Words such as *however, yet, still, nevertheless, but, instead of,* and *while* indicate an opposite meaning. *Skeptical* refers to "doubt or disbelief."

Punctuation marks following an unfamiliar word can also be important. Look especially for commas, parentheses, or dashes.

> Don suffered from a *phobia*—an irrational fear.

EXERCISE 3

Directions: For each sentence, use context clues to figure out the meaning of the italicized word. Write the meaning in the space provided.

1. Instead of being straightforward with his views, the candidate often *equivocates.*

   _____

2. In *The Bridge of San Luis Rey*, we learn about the characters through *flashbacks,* or the recalling of events from the past.

   _____

3. She was Leona's *surrogate* mother; that is, she replaced Leona's real mother.

   _____

4. Kathryn Kuhlman was blessed with *charisma*. She had the remarkable power of being able to heal people.

   _____

5. Today's computers include *modular* designs, a feature that allows you to add self-contained components or units to the basic system.

   _____

6. "An apple a day keeps the doctor away" is a famous *proverb,* yet few people know that Benjamin Franklin wrote this wise saying.

   _____

7. Martin Luther King, Jr., was the *bellwether* for the Civil Rights movement in the United States. He was the one who led African Americans on the road to equality.

   _____

8. The suspected carriers of the strange plague were in *quarantine,* which means they were effectively isolated from the rest of the hospital patients.

   _____

ANSWERS ARE ON PAGE 200.

WRITING ACTIVITY 1

Read these three words and their definitions.

monologue—a speech or dramatic sketch performed by one person

philanthropist—one who promotes the welfare of the human race, especially by giving huge donations

genealogy—the tracing of a person's ancestors or family tree

Choose one of the three words and write a descriptive paragraph in which you use the word you have chosen, but do not define it. Instead, provide as many context clues to its meaning as possible.

ANSWERS WILL VARY.

PRE-GED Practice
EXERCISE 4

Questions 1–8 refer to the following passage.

Bleached cow skulls remind one of Abiquiu's Georgia O'Keeffe, of wranglers, and hardship. And countless ristras, strands of blazing red chili
5 peppers, hung from ranch house porches, kindle the memory of New Mexico's fiery past.

First, there were prehistoric hunters, some as long as 11,500 years
10 ago. Later, Navajos and Apaches hunted deer and antelope, wove rugs, and painted pots eventually included among the world's collectibles. Next, the Spanish arrived. Compelled by rumors
15 of gold, Francisco Vasquez de Coronado rode up the Rio Grande from Mexico in 1540 with priests following close behind. By 1599, Juan de Onate, the first governor, was in office.

20 Finally, Anglo frontiersmen arrived from the East to tie their horses in plazas of towns whose older residents still today speak a Spanish which would be intelligible to Cervantes. From
25 Missouri to New Mexico, cowboys and longhorns suffered the rigors of the Santa Fe Trail.

The railroad ended an era when it pushed its pistons across the plains
30 beginning in 1880. Then as now, passengers who wanted to enjoy New Mexico's unpolluted, intoxicating air got off at Lamy, a hamlet as unchanged by time as Santa Fe's Palace of the
35 Governors, built in 1610.

—Excerpted from an article by Dennis Landt, *Home and Away* magazine

1. Which title best expresses the main idea of the passage?

    (1) The Spanish in New Mexico
    (2) The History of New Mexico
    (3) The Santa Fe Trail
    (4) Travel in New Mexico
    (5) New Mexico During the 19th Century

2. According to the passage, when did the first Spanish arrive in New Mexico?

    (1) 1599
    (2) 1800
    (3) with the railroad
    (4) before the Apaches and Navajos
    (5) after the Navajos and Apaches

3. Why did Coronado explore New Mexico?

    (1) to bring Christianity to the people
    (2) to take possession of new land
    (3) to find gold
    (4) to reach the Rio Grande
    (5) to find areas suitable for raising cattle

4. What are ristras?

    (1) bleached cow skulls
    (2) strands of chili peppers
    (3) ranch house porches
    (4) prehistoric hunters
    (5) Anglo frontiersmen

5. What is the main idea of the last paragraph?

    (1) The coming of the railroad marked the end of an era.
    (2) The railroads first pushed across the plains in 1880.
    (3) Pistons drive railroads.
    (4) New Mexico has clean air.
    (5) The buildings of Santa Fe are ancient.

6. A hamlet is a

    (1) railroad piston
    (2) palace of governors
    (3) settlement unchanged over time
    (4) train station
    (5) town with few people and clean air

7. What does New Mexico today have in common with the New Mexico of 1880?

    (1) fresh air
    (2) the Santa Fe trail
    (3) red chili peppers
    (4) deer and antelope
    (5) the Indian life

8. The first group to come to New Mexico were

    (1) Navajos
    (2) wranglers
    (3) Anglo frontiersmen
    (4) prehistoric hunters
    (5) Apaches

Questions 9–15 refer to the following passage.

The first thing I ever learned in the way of book knowledge was while working in this salt-furnace. Each salt-packer had his barrels marked with a

5 certain number. The number allotted to my stepfather was "18." At the close of the day's work the boss of the packers would come around and put "18" on each of our barrels, and I soon learned

10 to recognize that figure wherever I saw it, and after a while got to the point where I could make that figure, though I knew nothing about any other figures or letters.

15 From the time that I can remember having any thoughts about anything, I recall that I had an intense longing to learn to read. I determined, when quite a small child, that, if I accomplished

20 nothing else in life, I would in some way get enough education to enable me to read common books and newspapers. Soon after we got settled in some manner in our new cabin in

25 West Virginia, I induced my mother to get hold of a book for me. How or where she got it I do not know, but in some way she procured an old copy of Webster's "blue-back" spelling-

30 book, which contained the alphabet, followed by such meaningless words as "ab," "ba," "ca," "da." I began at once to devour this book, and I think that it was the first one I ever had in my

35 hands.

—Excerpted from *Up from Slavery,* by Booker T. Washington

9. What is the meaning of *induced* in line 25?

(1) helped
(2) persuaded
(3) allowed
(4) taught
(5) commanded

10. What is the best title for this passage?

    (1) How I Learned the Number "18"
    (2) My Early Education
    (3) My Job in the Salt-Furnace
    (4) The First Book I Owned
    (5) Pioneer Life in West Virginia

11. Which of the following had no influence on the author's early education?

    (1) the effect of memorizing the number "18" on salt barrels
    (2) the old copy of Webster's "blue-back" spelling book
    (3) his desire to learn to read
    (4) his desire to obtain a better job than his stepfather's
    (5) his mother's ability to get hold of a book for him

12. Washington obtained his first book knowledge when

    (1) he was working as a saltpacker
    (2) he moved to West Virginia
    (3) he obtained the dictionary
    (4) he first saw the alphabet
    (5) his stepfather showed him a newspaper

13. The word *procured* in line 28 has several meanings. What does the word mean in this story?

    (1) got possession of
    (2) took care of
    (3) brought about
    (4) achieved
    (5) accomplished

14. The word *devour* in line 33 has several meanings. What does the word mean in this story?

    (1) eat
    (2) destroy
    (3) enjoy greatly
    (4) prey upon
    (5) use up

15. The number "18" in this story signifies the

    (1) writer's age
    (2) number of saltpackers
    (3) number of barrels packed per day
    (4) number marked on the stepfather's barrels
    (5) age at which the writer learned to read

ANSWERS ARE ON PAGE 200.

2 Making Inferences

In Chapter 1, you learned how to identify main ideas, locate supporting details, and use context clues. These are essential skills for a literal understanding of what you read. But reading also involves inferential understanding.

INFERENCES

An *inference* is an educated guess about something that is not directly stated in a passage but is strongly hinted at or implied. For a complete understanding of written material, you must be able to make inferences wherever necessary.

When the main idea of a paragraph or a passage is not directly stated, you must infer it from whatever information is provided.

The main idea of the paragraph below is unstated. Notice, though, how the details help you infer what it is.

Some drove up in beat-up station wagons and dusty pickup trucks. Other, more citified types arrived in shiny convertibles or new campers. Cousin Otis Barnett, who owned half of the county, brought his family to the occasion in a private jet. Last, but not least, came Jack and Marge Barnett, oldest living members of the clan. They gladly volunteered details about their 22 great grandchildren.

The main idea of this passage is a family reunion. Did you correctly infer it? Four generations of an extended family—young and old, rich and poor—have gathered for a special occasion. You simply put the details together to come up with the main idea. Even the vocabulary helps you— *cousin, clan, great grandchildren.*

Use your inference skills to answer the questions based on the following passage.

Mom had come to live with us after my father-in-law died. With her came all of her huge pots and pans (she cooked for an army), her noodle machine, all her jars for canning, her pizzelle iron [a metal mold for making deep-fried desserts], her jars of roasted peppers, her
5 superlong rolling pin. Our house was transformed—you would open a closet door and get hit with a string of garlic. Inside several drawers, seeds were growing for something that would be planted later in the garden. On the counter was always a pot of water with lupini beans soaking.

10 And everywhere there was flour. She made noodles almost every day—just to pass the time, she would say. You would sit down and get up with flour all over your clothes. There was flour on the children, flour on the dog, flour choking all my plants, getting into all our lungs, threatening to kill us all. Sometimes I thought we were all the
15 filling in one big pasta.

—Excerpted from an article by Judy Esway,
New Covenant magazine

1. Who is Mom?

_____

2. Where would you most likely find Mom?

_____

3. How does the author feel about Mom?

_____

For question 1, Mom is the author's mother-in-law. You can infer this from the first sentence, which explains that Mom moved in after the author's father-in-law passed away. For question 2, Mom would be in the kitchen because she loves to cook. For question 3, the author regards Mom as an imposition, or someone who gets in the way. You can infer this from her complaints that Mom took over the kitchen, flour was everywhere, and family members seemed to become "all the filling in one big pasta."

EXERCISE 1

Directions: Read the passage below and answer the questions that follow.

They descended rapidly, directly over a large and imposing city in the middle of a vast, level, beautifully planted plain. While they were watching it, the city vanished and the plain was transformed into a heavily timbered mountain summit, the valleys falling away upon all sides as far as the eye could reach.

5 "Well, I'll say that's *some* mirage!" exclaimed Seaton, rubbing his eyes in astonishment. "I've seen mirages before, but never anything like that. Wonder what this air's made of? But we'll land, anyway, if we finally have to swim!"

The ship landed gently upon the summit, the occupants half expecting to see the ground disappear before their eyes. Nothing happened, however, and they disembarked, 10 finding walking somewhat difficult because of the great mass of the planet. Looking around, they could see no sign of life, but they *felt* a presence near them—a vast, invisible something.

Suddenly, out of the air in front of Seaton, a man materialized; a man identical with him in every detail, even to the smudge of grease under one eye, the small wrinkles in his 15 heavy blue serge suit, and the emblem of the American Chemical Society, which formed the pendant of his watch-fob.

—Excerpted from *The Skylark of Space*,
by E. E. Smith

1. Put a check in front of the statement that best summarizes the entire passage.

_____ **(1)** Seaton and his crew encounter strange events on a new planet.

_____ **(2)** Seaton meets his double on an unknown planet.

_____ **(3)** This city was located on a level, planted plain.

2. What effect does the disappearing city have on Seaton?

_____ **(1)** He is terrified.

_____ **(2)** He is astonished but persistent.

_____ **(3)** He can't decide what to do.

3. Which of the following can you infer about Seaton and the crew?

_____ **(1)** They need space suits to survive on the planet.

_____ **(2)** They want to turn back.

_____ **(3)** They are courageous.

ANSWERS ARE ON PAGE 201.

DRAWING CONCLUSIONS

Drawing a conclusion is a common type of inference skill. Suppose you and a friend decide to see a movie together. You agree to meet at the library at 7:00 P.M. and then walk to the movie, which starts at 7:30.

You arrive at the library at 6:45. At 7:10, your friend has still not arrived. By 7:30, you realize that your friend is not coming. You go home.

When you decide to go home, you are drawing a conclusion. Your friend has not actually told you anything, but, based on the fact that this person is half an hour late and the movie has started, you conclude that you have been stood up and that your friend is not coming.

≡ PRE-GED Practice ≡
EXERCISE 2

Questions 1–6 are based on the following conversation.

[IN A LOCAL BAR]

PAUL: Hey, Tom! Have a seat! Haven't seen you in a long time. How's it going?

5 TOM: I've just had the worst day of my life.

PAUL: How's that? [*Orders two beers*]

TOM: I just left the court. We split for good, me and the wife. 10 She got the kids, the house, everything.

PAUL: Sorry to hear that. [*Passes the pretzels*] I've been there, two years ago, you 15 know.

TOM: Yeah, at least your kids were grown. I've got little ones and a dead-end job.

20 PAUL: Being a welder isn't the end of the line.

TOM: When you pay big alimony it is. [*Pause*] She's living with lover boy, too.

PAUL: So kill her with kindness.

25 TOM: Are you crazy?

PAUL: I've learned that much. Love is bigger than anything. The hate will pass. And you'll feel better, too.

30 TOM: Impossible!

PAUL: Hang in there, Tom. I've got to get back to the office.

1. From this passage, you can infer that Paul is probably
   (1) younger than Tom
   (2) about the same age as Tom
   (3) older than Tom
   (4) Tom's brother
   (5) Tom's father

2. Which of the following jobs is Paul most likely to have?
   (1) insurance salesman
   (2) construction worker
   (3) teacher
   (4) druggist
   (5) auto mechanic

3. According to the passage, the source of Tom's troubles is that he
   (1) drinks too much
   (2) has a dead-end job
   (3) feels lonely
   (4) owes his wife money
   (5) got a divorce

4. From the conversation, you can conclude that Tom will probably
   (1) take Paul's advice
   (2) reject Paul's advice
   (3) think about Paul's advice
   (4) share Paul's advice
   (5) like Paul's advice

5. You can conclude that Tom
   (1) is pleased with his job
   (2) works in a courtroom
   (3) builds houses
   (4) makes a salary he is proud of
   (5) dislikes his job

6. You can conclude that *alimony* in line 21 means
   (1) court costs
   (2) house payments
   (3) support payments made to a spouse
   (4) home-improvement costs
   (5) school tuition costs

ANSWERS ARE ON PAGE 201.

APPLICATION OF IDEAS

Another kind of inference skill is the ***application of ideas***. This involves taking information from its source and applying it to another situation.

Stress is a human condition resulting from mental or physical strain. People facing new or difficult situations often experience stress.

According to the definition, put a check in front of the situation that would result in stress.

_____ **(1)** a walk in the park

_____ **(2)** a job interview

_____ **(3)** eating your favorite meal

Choice (2), a job interview, would result in stress.

You applied the definition of *stress* to a specific situation. The key words *new* and *difficult situations* helped you find the correct answer.

WRITING ACTIVITY 2

Imagine that you have just interviewed for a job you'd really like to get. Write a letter to the person who interviewed you. Say how much you appreciate being considered for the position. Emphasize your enthusiasm and your specific abilities to meet the employer's needs. Let the interviewer understand that you are interested and available immediately.

ANSWERS WILL VARY.

EXERCISE 3

Directions: Read the passage and answer the questions in the space provided.

Advertising plays a vital role in the nation's economy. Americans spend more than $33 billion a year on this enterprise. No other country invests in advertising as the United States does.

Advertising is found in media ranging from newspapers to outdoor signs. About 85
5 percent (or 85 cents out of every dollar) of newspaper advertising is done by local businesses and individuals. Radio receives about 70 percent of its advertising activity from the local community. National advertising is a favorite approach of mail-order houses. Magazines and television have great appeal to national advertisers.

The following chart shows the top three types of media for advertising and the
10 percentage of money spent on each.

Newspapers	30%	Television	20%
Direct mail	14%	All others	36%

Other forms of advertising include window displays, sale displays, and telephone directories. Novelties such as pencils, matchbooks, and business cards are inexpensive but useful advertising tools.

1. You want to sell your refrigerator. Where would you most likely place your ad?

_____

2. You are president of General Gadget Corporation. You want to tell the country about the latest in your new line of gadgets. Where would you advertise to reach the most people?

_____

3. The U.S. Postal Service has just delivered your favorite catalog. What kind of advertising is this?

_____

4. Out of every dollar spent on advertising, how many cents does television account for?

_____

ANSWERS ARE ON PAGE 201.

EXERCISE 4

Directions: Read the following ad. Then put a check in front of the correct answer to the questions that follow.

ALL TOYS DOLLS & GAMES PRICED $15.00 OR MORE

WITH THIS COUPON $5.00 OFF

SAT. — SUN.— MON.
Oct. 23, 24, & 25, 1994 at Emil's
Limit One Coupon Per Item, Sale Items
and Madame Alexander Dolls Not Included

1. For which of the following items can this coupon be used?

_____ **(1)** Wonderwoman, $12

_____ **(2)** Choo-Choo Game, $17

_____ **(3)** Pinata, $10

2. If you bought two items, how many coupons would you use?

_____ **(1)** none

_____ **(2)** one

_____ **(3)** two

3. This coupon can be used for all of the following EXCEPT

_____ **(1)** toys

_____ **(2)** dolls and games

_____ **(3)** sale items

ANSWERS ARE ON PAGE 201.

PRE-GED Practice
EXERCISE 5

Questions 1–4 are based on the following passage.

A Recycled Road

On Arizona's Interstate 10, I witnessed a major test of Mendenhall's discovery. A 22-mile stretch of pavement on I-10 had broken down in
5 both directions. By ordinary methods, repaving could cost millions of dollars for labor and virgin materials. But I saw three miles of an eastbound lane reborn in a single afternoon. Led by a
10 flagman, a huge road-eating machine that resembled a mechanical dinosaur came throbbing toward us. The machine traveled on enormous "caterpillar" tracks. Never pausing, it gobbled up the
15 old road. Whirling "shark's teeth" of carbon steel chewed the pavement to bean-size bits. Still advancing, the machine hurled them into passing trucks.

20 Load by load, what had been I-10 was rushed by an endless line of trucks to a nearby recycling plant, where technicians sprinkled it with softener. Quickly, I-10 came pouring back into
25 the trucks. Mile by mile, the recycled asphalt was dumped behind the retreating dinosaur and rolled flat in minutes by another machine.

By 5 P.M., cars and trucks were
30 rolling on a lovely reborn lane. Three months later, the entire 44 miles had been rebuilt. And scarcely a dollar had been spent for new asphalt.

—Excerpted from an article by
Edward Fales, *Reader's Digest*

1. Which special interest group would be most strongly opposed to using the new process?
   (1) trucking industry
   (2) suppliers of asphalt
   (3) highway contractors
   (4) heavy equipment manufacturers
   (5) environmentalists

2. The author's feelings about the topic are
   (1) cautious
   (2) negative
   (3) neutral
   (4) sarcastic
   (5) enthusiastic

3. Compared to other methods of highway construction, the Mendenhall discovery
   (1) is more economical
   (2) is more costly
   (3) is slower
   (4) needs more materials
   (5) needs more laborers

4. The word *recycled* (line 25) means
   (1) flattened
   (2) rolled
   (3) repaved
   (4) reused
   (5) inexpensive

ANSWERS ARE ON PAGE 201.

EXERCISE 6

Directions: Read the recipe and then answer the questions in the space provided.

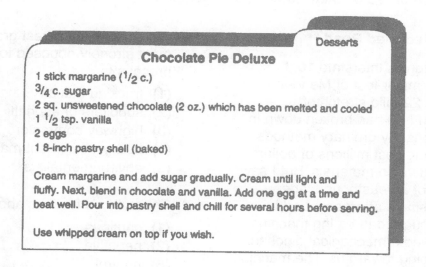

Desserts

Chocolate Pie Deluxe

1 stick margarine ($^1/_2$ c.)
$^3/_4$ c. sugar
2 sq. unsweetened chocolate (2 oz.) which has been melted and cooled
1 $^1/_2$ tsp. vanilla
2 eggs
1 8-inch pastry shell (baked)

Cream margarine and add sugar gradually. Cream until light and fluffy. Next, blend in chocolate and vanilla. Add one egg at a time and beat well. Pour into pastry shell and chill for several hours before serving.

Use whipped cream on top if you wish.

1. According to the recipe, what should be done right after the margarine and sugar are creamed until fluffy?

_____

2. How many eggs would you need for two pies?

_____

3. What is the next step after the eggs are beaten into the mixture?

_____

4. How much margarine equals one-half cup?

_____

ANSWERS ARE ON PAGE 201.

EXERCISE 7

Directions: Read the passage below. Circle *T* for each true statement, or *F* for each false statement.

The Great Depression

The Great Depression was a worldwide business slump of the 1930s. It ranked as the worst and longest period of high unemployment and low business activity in modern times. The Great Depression began in October 1929, when stock values in the United States dropped rapidly. Thousands of stockholders lost large sums of money. Many of
5   these stockholders were even wiped out. Banks, factories, and stores closed and left millions of Americans jobless and penniless. Many people had to depend on the government or charity to provide them with food.

President Herbert Hoover held office when the Great Depression began. The voters elected Franklin D. Roosevelt president in 1932. Roosevelt's reforms gave the government
10   more power and helped ease the depression.

The Great Depression ended after nations increased their production of war materials at the start of World War II. This increased level of production provided many jobs and put large amounts of money back into circulation.

The depression had lasting effects on the United States government and on many
15   Americans. For example, the government took more responsibility than ever before for strengthening the nation's economy. In addition, many Americans who lived during the depression stressed the importance in later years of acquiring such material comforts as household appliances and an automobile

—Excerpted from *The World Book Encyclopedia*

T F 1. "The Great Depression" is an appropriate title for this passage.

T F 2. The purpose of this passage is to criticize.

T F 3. According to the selection, Roosevelt's reforms helped the economy recover.

T F 4. From this passage, we can infer that hard times have a long-lasting effect.

ANSWERS ARE ON PAGE 201.

Questions 1–6 are based on the following passage.

Alone and Stranded

The words still echoed in my ears: "You're pregnant, about two months along." The doctor broke the news to me after my examination. She spoke
5 with a thick accent. I guessed that she was from India.

The people at the Community Clinic were very nice to me, especially the social worker. She told me about the
10 alternatives. I could keep the baby, have an abortion, or give it up for adoption.

They didn't know that my parents split up when I was fifteen. I ran away and met Larry. We lived together in
15 Uptown and ran errands for his "important" friends. Then I moved back with Mama after we had a fight.

I walked down Wilson Avenue back to the apartment. The heat brought
20 people out on the sidewalks, and they were hanging from the porches. I felt that they were staring at me.

I had to tell Larry what happened. I walked up the dark, musty stairway to
25 apartment 252A. I knocked and knocked, but he didn't answer. When I rang the office bell, I asked Sam where Larry was.

"Went to Texas, Sue. Left about
30 two nights ago. He took everything with him but the roaches. Y'know he still owes me back rent. Is there . . . is there anything I can do for you?" he asked with a startled look of concern.

35 I was shocked and turned away from Sam as I felt tears trickle down my face. Damn that Larry. Did he know too and then leave me?

I ran from the building and walked
40 to the lakefront until the locusts buzzed in the trees. They were there, yet I couldn't see them, just like my baby.

"Pregnant-pregnant," they seemed to say. Were they happy for me or were
45 they mocking me? I really couldn't tell.

1. According to the passage, which statement about the doctor is correct?

   (1) She is from India.
   (2) She wears thick glasses.
   (3) She has a thick accent.
   (4) She tells Sue about available alternatives.
   (5) She recommends adoption as the best alternative.

2. How does the news of the pregnancy affect the main character?

   (1) She is enthusiastic.
   (2) She appears indifferent.
   (3) She is self-assured.
   (4) She chooses to keep the baby.
   (5) She is confused and upset.

3. The author's attitude toward the young woman described in this passage could best be described as

   (1) indifferent
   (2) ironic
   (3) optimistic
   (4) arrogant
   (5) sympathetic

4. What can you infer about Sue's childhood and adolescence?

   (1) She was brought up in a happy home.
   (2) Her parents put Sue's needs ahead of theirs.
   (3) She and her family grew up in the South.
   (4) Sue was forced to grow up more quickly than usual.
   (5) As one of several children in her family, Sue didn't get enough attention.

5. What can you infer about Sue and Larry's relationship?

   (1) They love each other very much.
   (2) They enjoy living and working together.
   (3) They are not able to work out their problems with each other.
   (4) Larry is happy about Sue's pregnancy.
   (5) Larry wants Sue to give up the baby for adoption.

6. Why does Larry go to Texas?

   (1) He must find a job to support Sue and the coming baby.
   (2) He is behind on rent payments.
   (3) He can no longer live in their roach-infested apartment.
   (4) Larry knows about the pregnancy.
   (5) The passage does not say why he left.

ANSWERS ARE ON PAGE 201.

3 Analyzing Literature and the Arts Ideas

In this chapter, you will learn how to analyze passages, advertisments, and other materials you read. When you analyze something you read, you break it down into its parts to understand the whole. You will look at the patterns of organization writers use to present their ideas in a certain order. You will also study the types of words writers use (style) and the emotional bias often found in a piece of writing (tone).

Some of the ways materials are organized include the following patterns:

- order of importance
- sequence of events
- cause and effect
- comparison and contrast
- classification

ORDER OF IMPORTANCE

When presenting information according to its order of importance, you have two choices. Either you can build upward from a small detail to the central idea or you can work downward from the most important point. The following example starts with the most important point. The details that come next are progressively less important. The least important detail concludes the passage.

> The typical household budget includes many fixed expenses. Rent or mortgage payments rank among the highest expenditures. Next is the cost of food, always on the rise. Fuel bills also drain finances, especially during the heating season. Telephone, electricity, gas, and water cost less if families conserve usage. Finally, taxes, home and life insurance, and medical bills should be considered; they often entail only once- or twice-a-year obligations.

EXERCISE 1

Directions: Read the passage and then put a check in front of the correct answer to the questions that follow.

Small signs of a sugar binge [uncontrolled eating] were already there. As Vana opened the refrigerator, her eyes darted from the box of raisins to the leftover apple pie and back again. Then Vana gazed at the grapefruit. Before reaching for the melba toast in the cupboard, she gently fingered the package of sandwich cookies and the new
5 brownie mix. Although these distractions annoyed her, she felt cool and calm.

On her way out of the house, Vana sipped a can of diet cola. Fantasies about swimming in a chocolate shake drifted in and out of her head.

She felt herself weakening after she parked in the shopping center. Passing the bakery was too much. The sweet smells of freshly baked donuts and cakes greeted her
10 senses. Rows of pies, sweet rolls, and cookies beckoned. This was a rendezvous [meeting] with old friends. In that very hour, Vana devoured five glazed donuts and four brownies. The diet was over.

1. Which of the following details is the most important in the passage?

_____ **(1)** the fantasy about the milkshake

_____ **(2)** the binge at the bakery

_____ **(3)** the meal of grapefruit and melba toast

_____ **(4)** the cookies in the cupboard

2. In what order are the details presented?

_____ **(1)** least important to most important

_____ **(2)** most important to least important

ANSWERS ARE ON PAGE 202.

SEQUENCE OF EVENTS

Information is commonly organized according to a sequence-of-events approach. This approach lists events in the order in which they occurred. This approach is widely used in history, newspapers, and fiction. Recipes and instructions generally follow a sequence of events, too.

Certain words can help you spot a passage that is based on a sequence of events. These words include *first*, *second*, *third*, *finally*, *before*, *after*, *next*, and *then*.

Brown Leather Dye: Directions

Clean old polish and dirt from leather surface. Household cleaning fluid may be necessary. Shake well with top on. Remove top, invert bottle, press applicator against shoe. Apply liberally to badly scuffed areas first; then dye entire shoe. Apply two or more coats of dye if necessary. Let dry for 30 minutes between applications. After use, rinse applicator in water, blot dry, replace top. Dry shoes overnight before polishing or wearing them.

1. According to the directions, which sequence of steps is correct?

_____ **(1)** Apply dye liberally. Then remove old polish and dirt.

_____ **(2)** Dye entire shoe before applying dye to badly scuffed areas.

_____ **(3)** Dry shoes overnight before dyeing.

_____ **(4)** Dye entire shoe after applying dye to badly scuffed areas.

The correct sequence is given in choice (4), *Dye entire shoe after applying dye to badly scuffed areas.* Choice (1) is incorrect because the passage tells you to clean shoes before applying any dye. Choice (2) is the direct opposite of the correct sequence given in the passage. Choice (3) would be reasonable if shoes were soaked, but the passage does not address the matter of dyeing wet shoes.

EXERCISE 2

Directions: Read the following passage and answer the questions that follow.

Jake and the Bear

Old Jake Cochran was a gold miner. One night, while searching for gold in the high mountains of Canada, he made his camp by a stream. Near the stream he saw large tracks. He decided they probably belonged to a bear that had come to the stream to fish. Not wanting the animal in camp, he hung his food from a tree several yards from his tent
5   and his campfire.

Before dawn, Jake was awakened by a crashing sound. He leaped from his sleeping bag to peer out of his tent into the dim light. He saw the back of a huge, fur-covered creature rummaging through his food, which the creature had pulled down from the tree. Jake reached for his gun. First, the creature stood up and growled. Then, it turned around
10   to face Jake, looking more like a gigantic man than a bear. It stood upright like a man, but it must have weighed at least a thousand pounds, with thick, dark fur. After staring at Jake for what seemed like forever, the creature snatched some food in its front, pawlike hands, then disappeared into the brush with a few long strides.

1. In what order did the following events occur? Number them in correct sequence. The first one has been done for you.

_____ Jake was awakened by a noise.

_1_ Jake camped near a stream.

_____ The creature turned around and looked at Jake.

_____ Jake saw that a creature had pulled his food down from the tree.

_____ The manlike creature disappeared.

2. Given the sequence of events, what should Jake do next?

_____ (1) move his food into his tent

_____ (2) move his camp

_____ (3) call the police

ANSWERS ARE ON PAGE 202.

CAUSE AND EFFECT

Writers frequently use cause and effect to organize material. ***Causes***, or reasons, are presented together in one place. ***Effects***, or results, are grouped in another.

You are out walking alone one night. Just as you reach a dark yard bordered by a fence and dense hedges, a big German shepherd jumps into view, barking furiously. The scare almost takes your breath away. The sound of your footsteps (cause) has disturbed the dog (effect). The dog's furious barking (cause) scares you (effect).

Think about cause and effect as you read the following passage.

The National Character

Why did thousands of pioneers move west in the last century? Some settlers wanted more space because of rapid population growth in the East. Others like Kit Carson and Buffalo Bill yearned for an adventure. Many people rushed to stake out rich new farmland
5   or to claim a king's ransom in gold.

Even though these reasons were the most obvious ones for the movement west, the underlying basis for pioneering rests in the national character. Right up to the present day, Americans have taken pride in their rugged individualism. The settler's ability to overcome
10   obstacles with his or her own ingenuity was essential. Today, young Americans share this heritage in their affection for superheroes.

Look at the first line of the passage. Is westward migration presented as a cause or as an effect? Reread the first paragraph. Are the reasons for the westward migration presented as causes or as effects? In this passage, the effect (westward migration) is mentioned before the causes (desires for space, land, gold, and challenge). But, in fact, the effect resulted from the various causes. In real life, the causes came first.

Certain words can help you recognize a cause-and-effect passage. Look at the word *reasons* in the first line of the second paragraph. It is an important clue. It tells you that this passage is probably built around cause and effect. Other key terms that may indicate cause and effect include *cause, effect, due to, result, because, consequence, source, outcome, basis,* and *product.*

EXERCISE 3

Directions: Read the passage below. Circle *T* for each true statement, or *F* for each false statement.

Norberto's Secret

Every day after supper was done and the baby was asleep in his crib, Norberto and Carmen sat down to the work of the night. Husband and wife became student and teacher.

As a boy, Norberto had had little formal education. What schooling he did have was
5   poor. As he grew up, it became increasingly difficult for him to admit that he could not read. Instead, he just pretended to understand, keeping his unhappy secret to himself.

But when he met Carmen, he did not try to keep the secret from her. She understood and did not judge. She urged him to see a specialist at the reading clinic.

At first, Norberto resisted. He hated the thought of telling a stranger that he—a
10   father, a husband, a grown man—had never learned to read. But there was something he hated even more—being unable to read a story to the baby. A good father should be able to read his own son a bedtime story.

So Norberto began to study with Carmen at home. Once he learned how to read a little, he was not embarrassed to go to the clinic. The teachers there promptly saw how
15   determined he was. They were able to help him make maximum progress in minimum time.

T F 1. As a child, Norberto did not learn to read because his schooling was poor and irregular.

T F 2. Carmen helped Norberto because that's what the reading specialist advised.

ANSWERS ARE ON PAGE 202.

COMPARISON AND CONTRAST

Writers use ***comparison*** to show similarities and ***contrast*** to show differences. Apples and oranges are both fruits that grow on trees. They taste sweet and contain seeds. Because they are alike in these respects, we can compare their similarities.

But we can also contrast their differences. An apple is red and an orange is orange. An orange has a rough pebbly skin; an apple's skin is smooth. You can eat the skin of an apple, but orange peel is bitter.

Some passages use only comparison or only contrast. Others contain both. The following passage is about two brands of dog food.

PRIDE leads the pack!
Your pet knows the difference.

In nationwide taste tests, dogs of all breeds chose PRIDE over its closest competitor, Champ—67 percent to 33 percent.

5 Your canine friend will get the same nutritional value as with other brands. In fact, 100 percent of the daily requirements of vitamins and minerals goes into PRIDE.

The best part about PRIDE is the price. It's cheaper than Champ, but there's no difference in 10 weight or quality. Reward your dog with PRIDE, the premium dog food at a price you can afford.

1. According to the ad, which dog food is better?

_____

2. Compare the two brands.

_____

3. Contrast the two brands.

_____

The purpose of the ad is to persuade you that PRIDE is better. Comparison and contrast are both used to accomplish this.

The nutritional information, weight, and quality are presented as comparisons. In these respects, PRIDE is similar to its competition.

The taste and price information are presented as contrasts. Dogs like PRIDE better. PRIDE is cheaper. When it comes to flavor and economy, PRIDE and the competition are nothing alike. They are quite different, and the differences favor PRIDE.

Certain key terms can help you recognize passages of comparison and contrast. These include: *compare, contrast, more than, comparison, differ, less than, alike, different, prefer, similar, on the other hand, larger, smaller, on the one hand, although, same, equal, better than, worse than,* and *both.*

EXERCISE 4

Directions: Read the following passage and then answer the questions in the space provided.

Running for Office

Lopez   Gates

Peter Lopez and John Gates are running for district representative this November. Each man has striking similarities to the other, yet there are profound differences between them.

5   Pete and John both come from the west end of Elmwood. However, John now lives in the affluent Oak Hills section, while Pete still occupies the plain frame house where he was born. Both candidates were star basketball players at Elmwood High School. They also served in 10   the Vietnam War. Pete and John believe strongly in their community and in their country, but Pete is a Democrat and John a Republican.

On the one hand, Pete Lopez identifies closely with the blue-collar workers and the average citizen. He is a steelworker who supports the rights of the man on the street. He has the support of labor unions and many working-class blacks, Mexicans, and Irish 15   who live in the district.

On the other hand, John Gates receives his backing from professionals, some white-collar workers, farmers, and businesspeople of the area. A self-made millionaire in real estate, Gates gets large donations from his wealthy backers in business.

Both candidates promise the same things: better jobs, better schools, better roads, 20   and better lives for citizens in the district. If elected, would either actually keep his promises?

1. How are Pete and John similar?

_____

2. What campaign promises do both candidates make?

_____

3. How are Pete and John different?

_____

ANSWERS ARE ON PAGE 202.

CLASSIFICATION

To *classify* information means to put it into categories that enhance understanding. Political candidates, for example, can be classified according to such factors as the office they are seeking, their party identification, and their state or district.

Classification is used in the following list of jobs showing the qualifications, salary, and employment outlook for each job.

Occupation	Training and Requirements	Salary Range	Employment Outlook
Auto Mechanic	on-the-job; vocational school; apprenticeship	$19,000–20,000	VG
Licensed Practical Nurse	1 yr. voc. school; 1 yr. hospital training	$13,800–17,600	VG
Machinist	4-yr. apprenticeship	$14,000–21,000	A/G
Postal Clerk	written exam, high school helpful	$14,600–21,000	NG
Secretary	high school or business school	$13,000–20,000	G/VG

1. Which job has the highest starting salary?

_____

2. Which job requires a 4-year apprenticeship?

_____

3. What is the outlook for postal clerks?

_____

For question 1, the *auto mechanic* has the highest starting salary. For question 2, a *machinist* must serve a 4-year apprenticeship. For question 3, the job outlook for postal clerks is *not good* (*NG*).

≡ PRE-GED Practice ≡
EXERCISE 5

Questions 1–3 refer to the following passage.

In My Son's Bedroom

Before adults go to sleep, they usually read, watch television, or listen to the radio. It's all very conventional. What a child uses to promote slumber
5   [sleep] is a real surprise.

Take my nine-year-old, for instance. Here is a list of things I found in his bed one night. The first thing I saw was his collection of toys. His toy
10 car lay overturned near the pillow. Spiderman was still battling the Star Trek spaceship, and two walkie-talkie batteries stood lonely and forlorn on the bedpost.

15 As I rearranged the blankets, all kinds of Halloween candy spilled on the floor. There were leftover Tootsie Rolls, Life Savers, and pieces of bubble gum. Mars bars wrappers littered the sheets
20 like fallen leaves. Never one to neglect his schooling, my sleepyhead cuddled up to his world globe with nose pointed north. In the educational grouping, I also found one stubby pencil and The
25 Book of Lost Treasure.

Finally, in the mixed category, I uncovered two volcanic rocks from our trip to Arizona and one cowboy hat from Yellowstone National Park. As I turned
30 off the light, I gently pulled a dirty sock from under his arm. I kissed him good-night and returned to my adult world.

1. According to the passage, in which category is the world globe?
   (1) toys
   (2) candy
   (3) education
   (4) travel
   (5) mystery

2. Which of the following would be in the mixed category?
   (1) pencil
   (2) walkie-talkie batteries
   (3) bubble gum
   (4) dirty sock
   (5) Spiderman

3. In which category are the two batteries?
   (1) toys
   (2) candy
   (3) education
   (4) travel
   (5) mystery

ANSWERS ARE ON PAGE 202.

STYLE AND TONE

Style and tone refer to the way writers use words. *Style* refers to particular types of words and sentences. Writing styles can be formal or informal, flowery or concise, dramatic, and poetic. Let's examine three styles of communication.

"Thanks for your help. You did a super job on our house." (*Informal*)

"Thank you for your assistance. Your work on our house was of the highest quality." (*Formal*)

"Your invaluable assistance has been most deeply appreciated. The fruits of your labor are sure to astound all who enter our abode." (*Flowery*)

As you can see, there are real differences among these styles; however, the basic message is the same: "You did a good job!" An informal style is characterized by short, simple words and sentences. A more formal style uses more difficult words and longer sentences. A flowery style uses very fancy words in long, winding sentences.

Tone refers to emotion. Tone may be serious or humorous, sad or happy, angry or pleasant. A writer with an optimistic outlook on a subject uses a bright, upbeat tone. A gloomy tone is likely to characterize an article by a writer with a pessimistic point of view.

Learn to recognize irony and sarcasm. *Irony* is a type of writing that implies that something is not what it appears to be. When people speak ironically, they say the opposite of what they mean. The million-dollar-lottery winner who says, "All this money lying around is a bit of a nuisance," is speaking ironically. *Sarcasm* is a tone of bitter humor. It is usually directed at a particular target. Here are the reactions of two passengers during a turbulent flight.

Passenger 1: "I haven't had so much fun since kindergarten."

Passenger 2: "Where'd they find this flight crew, anyway? The circus?"

The two passengers react in quite different ways. The first passenger takes an ironic tone, finding the whole situation more amusing than anything else. The second passenger is plainly sarcastic. The tone of bitterness toward the crew is unmistakable.

EXERCISE 6

Directions: Read the passage below and then put a check in front of the correct answer to the questions that follow.

A Driver's Nightmare

It was an evil night to be driving. The wind drove the rain in great sheets onto the windshield. The wipers could not keep up with the downpour.

Cheri drove slowly. She had left her last client late and probably should have stayed in town, but Sal had demanded that she drive on to Union City. That way, she would be
5   there for the breakfast appointment with a new client.

Suddenly Cheri slammed on her brakes.

"What was that? I thought I saw something in the road. Someone crouching. I must have imagined it. Whoa, I must be tired . . . talking to myself."

Cheri had increased her speed again when she heard a pop. The car swerved
10 savagely to the right.

"Oh, no . . . not a flat . . . not tonight—I don't even have a spare." The car rolled to a stop near a ditch. She felt for her flashlight, found it in the glove compartment, and got out of the car. The flashlight beam came to rest on the tire, sagging useless against the soggy ground.

15 "Better try to find help."

Cheri looked through the black trees that lined the road. Somewhere to her left, she heard a dog howl.

Her flashlight stabbed the darkness. She walked back down the road, head down against the driving rain. Then she saw the row of nails on the road. She could see the
20 place where her tires had disturbed them. Someone had deliberately placed a straight line of nails across the right lane.

Her eyes widened in fear. A cold knot gripped her stomach. She began to run, blindly.

1. The style of lines 7–8 can best be described as

_____ **(1)** formal

_____ **(2)** emotional

_____ **(3)** informal

2. What is the overall tone of the passage?

_____ **(1)** ironic

_____ **(2)** tense

_____ **(3)** angry

ANSWERS ARE ON PAGE 202.

EXERCISE 7

Directions: Read the speech below and then answer the questions that follow in the space provided.

Citizens!

It is now time for the people of this country to unite themselves under the banner of comradeship, to establish a strong front against the ills that beset us all. When each person acts solely for his or her own best interest, the masses suffer. When all people work together for the common good, they all profit. I ask all people to work for the common good.

1. The style of this passage is _____.

2. The tone of this passage is _____.

ANSWERS ARE ON PAGE 202.

WRITING ACTIVITY 3

Write one short classified advertisement in paragraph form for one of these categories: apartments for rent, used cars for sale, child-care services.

Limit your ad to one paragraph. Don't use abbreviations. Just write several descriptive sentences about the specific product or service you are advertising. Make sure to include the kinds of detail a prospective customer would want to know before responding to your ad.

ANSWERS WILL VARY.

EXERCISE 8

Directions: Study the book list below and then put a check in front of the correct answer to the questions that follow.

Books to Read

Level I

Daugs, Richard. *The Golden Years: Fit for Life*. Gallery Books, 1990. Gives tips on exercise, finances, and getting new interests.

Falk, Ursula A. *On Your Own: Independent Living for Older Persons*. Prometheus, 1989. Provides insights into the stresses of loneliness, finances, and physical security.

Friedan, Betty. *The Fountain of Age*. Simon & Schuster, 1993. Distinguishes what is irreversible after 40 from what remains open to choice and vitality.

Larue, Gerald A. *Gereoethics: A New Vision of Growing Old in America*. Prometheus, 1992. Assesses the impact of societal values on the elderly and how they may respond to them.

Solomon, David H., et al., eds. *A Consumer's Guide to Aging*. Johns Hopkins University Press, 1992.

Level II

Berman, Phillip L., ed. *The Courage to Grow Old*. Ballantine, 1989. Presents inspirational essays on the philosophies of aging by 41 prominent men and women.

Cole, Thomas R. *The Journey of Life: A Cultural History of Aging in America*. Cambridge University Press, 1992.

Rountree, Cathleen. *On Women Turning 50*. HarperSanFrancisco, 1993. Profiles of 18 women over 50 from the fields of politics, science, education, business, and the arts.

Swisher, Karin, ed. *The Elderly: Opposing Viewpoints*. Greenhaven, 1990. Uses magazines, books, and position papers for a wide range of individuals and organizations.

Vierck, Elizabeth. *Fact Book on Aging*. ABC-CLIO, 1990. Presents hundreds of facts from housing and health care to travel and community involvement for people who are 65 and over.

1. How are the entries arranged in the two lists?

_____ **(1)** in alphabetical order by author

_____ **(2)** alphabetically by title

_____ **(3)** alphabetically by publisher

2. Which author presents profiles of individuals over the age of 50?

_____ **(1)** Rountree

_____ **(2)** Vierck

_____ **(3)** Friedan

3. When was the newest book on the list published?

_____ **(1)** 1992

_____ **(2)** 1993

_____ **(3)** 1994

4. Which author would you recommend to an elderly person confronting a personal fear of aging?

_____ **(1)** Solomon

_____ **(2)** Berman

_____ **(3)** Cole

5. Which book presents ideas on exercise and finances?

_____ **(1)** *A Consumer's Guide to Aging*

_____ **(2)** *Fact Book on Aging*

_____ **(3)** *The Golden Years: Fit for Life*

ANSWERS ARE ON PAGE 202.

EXERCISE 9

Directions: Read the following passage. Circle *T* for each true statement, or *F* for each false statement.

Taming the Wind

The problem of billowing skirts in windy plains country was no minor one, and though it was met and overcome, there is some evidence that the solution was the work of a male—none other than our old friend, George Armstrong Custer. When the Custers went to Fort Riley after the Civil War, Elizabeth's dresses were all "five yards around, and
5 gathered as full as could be into the waistband." On her first walk across the windy prairie ground, her skirt billowed like a balloon, flew out in front, then lifted over her head. His military dignity thus affronted, George immediately figured out a way to keep his wife's skirts at their proper level. He cut some lead bars into strips and ordered Elizabeth to sew them into the hems of her dresses. Thus weighted down, she was able to outwit the
10 elements while taking her constitutionals about the post. Other women followed her example, and a dozen years later all were wearing bar lead in their skirt hems on the windy western plains.

—Excerpted from *The Gentle Tamers*, by Dee Brown

T F 1. The style of the passage is best described as military.

T F 2. The tone of the passage is critical.

T F 3. When Elizabeth Custer first walked across the windy prairie, her skirts were wildly blown about.

T F 4. Other women followed Elizabeth's example.

T F 5. George Custer's idea was for women to weight their skirts down with metal strips.

T F 6. Another word for *constitutionals* is *walks*.

T F 7. The material in Mrs. Custer's dress measured about three yards at the waistband.

T F 8. The other women on the plains laughed at Custer's absurd idea.

ANSWERS ARE ON PAGE 202.

☰ PRE-GED Practice ☰
EXERCISE 10

Questions 1–12 on the next two pages are based on the following passage.

Aunt Rosie's Advice

"Anger is just hurt covered over," Aunt Rosie had said. "If you want to solve the problem, stay in touch with the hurt. Don't let the anger take over,
5   or you'll never get anything worked out. The ego uses anger to build a fence around itself so it won't get hurt again."

I heard the click of the door. "Stay in touch with the hurt," I told myself.

10   I thought about her advice. Les was late again. He'd said he'd be home by six. It was nearly 8:30.

Les stood hesitantly, as if I were going to throw something.

15   "Sorry I'm late," he said softly. He had tired lines around his eyes and mouth. His shoulders drooped.

"I felt really hurt that you weren't here when you said you would be. I
20   fixed a really nice dinner, but it's all cold now," I said.

"I'm sorry. I couldn't even call. The boss insisted I go out to that new construction site and settle the change
25   of plans with the foreman. I couldn't even get to a phone to call you . . . thanks for not being mad."

Aunt Rosie was right, I thought. If I had hit him full tilt with anger, we'd have
30   just had a big fight. I smiled at him.

"Well, it can't be undone now, I guess," I told him. I wasn't feeling angry anymore.

Les put down his briefcase and
35   drew me into his arms. "Tell you what," he said, "How 'bout Friday night, we'll go out to eat—just to make up for tonight's ruined dinner."

"OK," I agreed. Then to myself I
40 said, "Thanks, Aunt Rosie, you were
right. If you want to solve the problem,
don't let anger take over. Stay in touch
with the hurt."

1. According to Aunt Rosie, what is the
   best way to prevent problems in a
   relationship?

   (1) Don't let anger take over.
   (2) Control the hurt.
   (3) Call when you're going to be late.
   (4) Get your anger out into the open.
   (5) Stay in touch with your partner's
       feelings.

2. Which inference CANNOT be drawn
   from the passage?

   (1) Aunt Rosie is a busybody.
   (2) Aunt Rosie is a wise woman.
   (3) The author loves her husband.
   (4) Les did not intend to make his wife
       angry.
   (5) Adults can learn to change their
       patterns of behavior.

3. What is the main idea of the passage?

   (1) Inconsiderate behavior can destroy
       a marriage.
   (2) Aunt Rosie can't resist interfering.
   (3) Anger is pain in disguise.
   (4) The author is overworked.
   (5) Les is overworked.

4. Suppose a neighbor carelessly trampled
   some flowers you had just planted.
   What would Aunt Rosie most likely
   advise you to do?

   (1) Say nothing and plant new flowers.
   (2) Confront the neighbor and demand
       to know how a person could be so
       careless.
   (3) Send the neighbor a letter
       requesting that the person replace
       the flowers that were destroyed.
   (4) Insist that the neighbor repay you
       what the flowers cost.
   (5) Quietly tell the neighbor how this
       carelessness has upset you.

5. What is the style of this passage?

   (1) poetic
   (2) flowery
   (3) informal
   (4) dramatic
   (5) formal

6. According to Aunt Rosie, the expression
   of anger results in

   (1) divorce
   (2) solving problems
   (3) staying in touch with the hurt
   (4) nothing productive
   (5) clearing the air

7. There was no big fight because

   (1) Les finally came home on time, for a change
   (2) the author expressed her disappointment calmly and truthfully
   (3) the boss let Les call home
   (4) Aunt Rosie intervened
   (5) the couple went out to dinner

8. What expression of feeling did Les expect from his wife when he came home late from work?

   (1) fear
   (2) anger
   (3) calm acceptance
   (4) amusement
   (5) understanding

9. Les came home late from work because he

   (1) went out for a drink with friends
   (2) stayed in the office to catch up on his work
   (3) felt hurt about a previous argument
   (4) had to do work for his boss
   (5) made a habit of working late each night

10. From the passage, you can infer that Les may be a(n)

    (1) construction worker
    (2) real estate agent
    (3) architect
    (4) landscaper
    (5) retail salesperson

11. How would you describe Les's frame of mind as he came home late from work?

    (1) angry and confused
    (2) sorry and hesitant
    (3) hurt and depressed
    (4) belligerent and angry
    (5) calm and happy

12. How would you characterize the writer's tone?

    (1) optimistic
    (2) angry
    (3) confused
    (4) gloomy
    (5) amused

ANSWERS ARE ON PAGE 203.

UNDERSTANDING LITERATURE AND THE ARTS

■ Nonfiction Prose
■ Prose Fiction
■ Poetry
■ Drama
■ Commentaries on the Arts

4 Nonfiction Prose

In this chapter, you will study nonfiction prose. The subjects include real people, places, events, and social issues. When you read a newspaper or a magazine, an essay or a speech, a biography or an account of a true experience, you are reading nonfiction prose.

READING NONFICTION PROSE

News articles and feature stories are the most common kinds of nonfiction prose. News articles report breaking events—a fire, a robbery, or an election result. They are built around the five Ws: *who, what, when, where,* and *why*. The key information is presented first.

When reading straight news, ask yourself:

- Who or what is the subject of the story?

- What happened?

- When and where did the events take place?

- Why did they occur?

Features are not as limited by time as straight news is. They can examine almost any subject of general interest. Breaking news is often the starting point for feature pieces. But features can also stand perfectly well by themselves.

EXERCISE 1

Directions: Read the nonfiction selection below. Circle *T* for each true statement, or *F* for each false statement.

Covenant House, New York City

Covenant House offers shelter to over 20,000 homeless youths each year who roam 42nd Street. It is a place where the young runaways and delinquents of Times Square can find sanctuary and hope.

Sister Rose McGeady is the director. With a staff of 70 full-time workers and almost
5 200 part-timers, she keeps Covenant House open 24 hours a day. No child is ever turned away.

In the dangerous world of 42nd Street, sex and drugs are big business. Pimps, drug dealers, and pornography hustlers lure young people into crime with cruel promises of money and security.

10 The children who turn up at Covenant House tell horror stories of life on the street. An 11-year-old explains how he was given a new video game for spending a night as a male prostitute. A 14-year-old says her first job was acting in a pornographic movie. A friend of hers was stabbed to death after refusing to shoot heroin with a customer.

Covenant House offers help to young victims of crime and indifference. Runaways
15 receive food, clothing, shelter, medical care, counseling, and job training. "It's a fresh start," says one 16-year-old who, a month ago, was running away from neighborhood gangs. "A fresh start in a safe place."

T F 1. Covenant House is located in Times Square.

T F 2. Criminals lure teenage runaways with offers of money.

T F 3. Covenant House is one of 70 shelters for homeless children in the 42nd Street area.

T F 4. The purpose of the article is to present a profile of the director.

T F 5. The youngest child mentioned in the article was 9 years old.

T F 6. The child who was knifed to death had once been turned away from Covenant House.

T F 7. The full-time staff at Covenant House numbers almost 200.

T F 8. In the street world of drugs and sex for sale, teenage delinquents all too often find sanctuary.

ANSWERS ARE ON PAGE 203.

EXERCISE 2

Directions: Read the selection below, which combines science and history to report new findings about the death of the emperor Napoleon. Then answer the questions that follow.

The French emperor Napoleon died in 1821, in the prime of his life. One of the most powerful European leaders of all time, he ended his days in exile, a tragic figure. History tells us that the cause of his death was stomach cancer. But recent evidence suggests that he was murdered.

5   In the book *The Murder of Napoleon,* Sten Forshufvud, a Swedish author, makes a strong case that Napoleon was poisoned by his longtime rival and fellow officer, Count Charles Tristan de Montholon.

The evidence points to arsenic poisoning over a period of five or six years. The autopsy revealed an enlarged liver, a telltale sign of arsenic overdose. Records indicate

10   that, while in exile on the island of St. Helena, Napoleon showed symptoms of chronic arsenic poisoning. Family members reported that he complained of sleepiness, insomnia, swollen feet, and excessive weight gain.

Dr. Forshufvud chemically analyzed strands of Napoleon's hair that relatives had saved. The analysis showed abnormally high traces of arsenic.

15   The most startling evidence of murder actually came to light in 1840. Napoleon's body was moved to Paris. When the coffin was opened, observers were shocked to see a well-preserved body instead of bones and dust. One of the most unusual effects of arsenic is that it greatly slows the decay of living tissue.

1. According to Dr. Forshufvud, what was the cause of Napoleon's death?

_____

2. What symptoms of arsenic poisoning did Napoleon have?

_____

3. How did the autopsy results support Dr. Forshufvud's theory?

_____

4. What is the strongest evidence that Napoleon died of arsenic poisoning?

_____

5. What chemical analysis did Dr. Forshufvud perform?

_____

6. Where did Napoleon spend the last years of his life? Why?

_____

ANSWERS ARE ON PAGE 203.

EXERCISE 3

Directions: Read the passage below. Circle *T* for each true statement, or *F* for each false statement.

For centuries, venereal diseases (VD) have afflicted king and commoner alike and may even have changed the course of history. Henry VIII and Ivan the Terrible are only two of the rulers now believed to have had syphilis and to have suffered from its complications.

5   When antibiotics were discovered, many thought that the problem of venereal diseases had been solved.

Such has not been the case. Recent VD increases around the world have indicated that the traditional methods of control—treatment with drugs and tracing an infected person's sexual contacts for treatment—have not been completely effective. Some

10   organisms that cause VD have become increasingly drug resistant and, like other infections, venereal diseases are often transmitted before symptoms occur and treatment is begun.

The National Institute of Allergy and Infectious Diseases (NIAID) several years ago began a program in research on sexually transmitted diseases—primarily syphilis and

15   gonorrhea. These studies are carried out by grant- and contract-supported investigators at institutions around the country.

The NIAID program is based on the opinion of experts who believe that a better basic understanding of all sexually transmitted diseases and of the organisms causing them must be developed before there can be improvement in methods of prevention or

20   therapy.

T F 1. According to the passage, improvement in the treatment of venereal diseases lies in greater use of drug therapy.

T F 2. NIAID's position is that, before there can be substantial improvement in the treatment of venereal diseases, there must be more effective tracing of the sexual contacts of infected persons.

T F 3. The National Institute of Allergy and Infectious Diseases is calling for a better basic understanding of sexually transmitted diseases and their causes.

T F 4. The word *complications* at the end of the first paragraph most likely refers to negative effects.

T F 5. It can be inferred from the passage that some venereal diseases are becoming more difficult to treat.

ANSWERS ARE ON PAGE 203.

FACTS AND OPINIONS

The ability to distinguish fact from opinion is an important skill. A *fact* can be proved by observation or research. An **opinion** is a personal judgment or belief. Look at the following statements.

Fact: The first American president to resign from office was Richard Nixon.

Opinion: Politicians are all dishonest.

Fact: The United States and Russia possess more nuclear weapons than any other nation.

Opinion: Nuclear weapons will eventually destroy all life on Earth.

Opinions can be introduced with such phrases as *I feel, I think, I believe, in my opinion,* and *from my viewpoint.*

Read the paragraph below and answer the questions that follow in the space provided.

(1) Yesterday, I went to Thrifty's Food Store. **(2)** It seems to me that Thrifty's is the cheapest supermarket in town. **(3)** I noticed that Cluck's Chicken Soup is ten cents less there than at Buy Right. **(4)** Fancy Farms Whole Wheat Bread is two cents a loaf cheaper than at Buy Right. **(5)** Thrifty's offers the best value.

1. Which sentences in the passage are facts? Write the numbers.

_____

2. Which sentences in the passage are opinions? Write the numbers.

_____

Sentences (1), (3), and (4) are facts. They name the stores and give specific prices. Sentences (2) and (5) are the personal opinions of the shopper. The words *cheapest* and *best* signal that personal opinions are being stated.

EXERCISE 4

Directions: Read the passage below and then put a check in front of the correct answer to the questions that follow.

A high school diploma or a high school equivalency diploma is vital for success in today's society. One manager at a large company says that he won't hire a person without a diploma. The military wants enlistees to have completed formal education before beginning active duty. Training schools and colleges require applicants to have a
5 high school diploma.

Adults 18 and older can earn a high school diploma through home study or at adult education centers. More than one million adults do so each year. Of these, more than two-thirds pass the five tests required for a high school equivalency diploma, more commonly known as the GED.

10 I believe one student put it best when he said that the GED offered him a second chance at life. Another explained that a terrible burden had been lifted from her shoulders.

"No doubt about it. My GED made all the difference," declared a recently promoted office worker.

1. Which of the following statements is based on information in the passage?

_____ **(1)** You can't get a job without a high school diploma.

_____ **(2)** A high school diploma increases a person's chances for success.

_____ **(3)** The military will not accept dropouts.

2. According to the selection, which of the following is a fact?

_____ **(1)** More than one million adults try to complete their high school education each year.

_____ **(2)** Most employers require at least a high school education.

_____ **(3)** Most people earn a GED to feel better about themselves.

3. Which of the following is the author's opinion?

_____ **(1)** Training schools and colleges cater to high school graduates.

_____ **(2)** A GED certificate offers a second chance for many adults.

_____ **(3)** Employers place too much emphasis on qualifications.

4. The graduate who was quoted

_____ **(1)** had recently been promoted

_____ **(2)** served in the military

_____ **(3)** had no opinion

ANSWERS ARE ON PAGE 203.

DETECTING AN AUTHOR'S BIAS

Authors' personal opinions can give their writing a positive or negative slant, called a *bias*. Biased writing stresses certain facts and omits others. It makes assertions that are unsupported by facts. Its purpose is to influence the reader toward a particular point of view. Writing that is intended to influence people without their being aware of it is called *propaganda*.

Read each selection below. Write *balanced* if it appears to be truthful and fair. Write *biased* if it distorts or slants information.

1. Buy Wonder Vitamin C today. It's better for you than oranges. Just pop a tablet into your mouth and enjoy the refreshing taste.

_____

2. The City Council meeting broke up after a lengthy debate. The woman's supporters argued that she was the duly elected representative of the people and should be allowed to take her seat on the council. Her opponents disputed this, saying that her previous disruptions of council activities disqualified her from holding public office.

_____

3. There is still controversy about the future of the space program. While critics say it diverts much-needed funds away from social programs, supporters point to the great scientific advances that have resulted from the exploration of space. The widespread use of micro-processors is one major result of space-related research.

_____

4. Do you want the federal government to tax your savings income? Senior citizens will be hurt by this proposed legislation. Don't let greedy Uncle Sam pocket more of your hard-earned money. Write to your representative and senators today.

_____

Statement 1 is *biased*. The ad is slanted in favor of a commercial product. It claims the vitamin C tablet is superior to oranges. Statement 2 is *balanced*. The author describes what happened and sticks to the facts, offering no personal opinions about either position. Statement 3 is *balanced*. This is a factual explanation of two opposing views of the space program. The author discusses others' opinions but does so in a balanced manner. Statement 4 is *biased*. The author says that the government is greedy and will pocket taxes from the savings of senior citizens. No facts are given to support this.

EXERCISE 5

Directions: As you read the selection below, look for the author's biases. Then put a check in front of the correct answer to the questions that follow.

Do you enjoy your diet when you are trying to lose weight fast? On a low-carbohydrate diet, you give up bread, spaghetti, cake—all the good things in life. On a low-protein diet, you're anemic without steak and homesick for ham. A low-fat diet means turning away from cheddar cheese and chocolate ice cream.

With the Easy Diet Program, you can enjoy life while you peel off the pounds. You simply mix half a cup of Easy Diet Formula in a glass of water, put the mixture into the blender, and sip away your worries. Enjoy the sweet, rich flavor of a milk shake while getting all your daily nutritional requirements. Drink the formula three times a day and lose weight the Easy Diet way!

1. The writer mentions the low-carbohydrate, low-protein, and low-fat diets to

_____ **(1)** present their good points

_____ **(2)** inform the reader

_____ **(3)** emphasize the advantages of the Easy Diet Program

2. Which of the following best illustrates the use of biased language?

_____ **(1)** "You're anemic without steak and homesick for ham."

_____ **(2)** "You give up bread, spaghetti, cake."

_____ **(3)** "Mix half a cup of Easy Diet Formula in a glass of water."

ANSWERS ARE ON PAGE 203.

NEWSPAPERS AND PERIODICALS

Newspapers provide up-to-date information about news in local areas and around the world. They inform people about a wide variety of topics, such as politics, sports, human interest stories, and entertainment. Millions of people read a daily or weekly newspaper so they can stay informed about current events.

Periodicals (magazines) are usually published by the week or month. Unlike newspapers, they tend to specialize in a certain topic. You might find a column on hunting or fishing in your local paper, but for an in-depth look at these subjects, you would turn to a magazine such as *Outdoor Life* or *Field and Stream*.

EXERCISE 6

Directions: Read the passage below and answer the questions that follow.

Ever since Israel became independent in 1948, it has had unusual educational needs. Two factors account for this.

First, Israel's topography [land] is inhospitable [harsh]. Much of the country is desert or mountainous. Second, Israel is always in a state of military alert because of border
5   disputes with neighboring countries.

Though this nation of four million has regular primary and secondary schools, the *Nahal* has evolved as a unique educational unit for the special needs of border settlements. The *Nahal* is a branch of the military. Unlike traditional schools, it offers a curriculum composed of military training and cooperative agriculture. It stresses loyalty
10   and social responsibility to the state. In addition to required courses, students can also take dancing, Hebrew, and folksinging.

The basic structural unit of the *Nahal* is the *garin,* a group of young people serving in the army together. Their education begins with basic infantry training. After they learn soldiering, they join a *kibbutz,* a collective farm, to work as farmers on the frontier.

15   A *garin's* military training never ends. Settlements are always in danger of attack. After months of army training, the members of the *garin* return to civilian life as soldier-farmers.

Match the terms listed on the left with their definitions on the right. Write the correct letter on the line.

_____ **1.** topography   **(a)** the courses that make up a program of study

_____ **2.** inhospitable   **(b)** a place's physical landscape

_____ **3.** *Nahal*   **(c)** barren and rough

_____ **4.** curriculum   **(d)** an educational unit of the Israeli military

_____ **5.** *garin*   **(e)** a group of young soldiers who are trained and educated together

_____ **6.** *kibbutz*   **(f)** a collective farm

_____ **7.** civilian   **(g)** someone who is not in the military

ANSWERS ARE ON PAGE 204.

EDITORIALS

Editorials are the opinions of newspapers. One newspaper's stand on an issue can be the opposite of another's. A paper's opinion usually appears on the editorial page so that readers do not confuse it with straight news.

A straight news story about an election, for example, would report the positions that the candidates represent. But an editorial might urge readers to vote for one candidate instead of another.

EXERCISE 7

Directions: Read the editorial below and then put a check in front of the correct answer to the questions that follow.

The city council is debating a ban on the ownership of handguns by private citizens. Supporters argue that one out of every two homicides here is committed with a handgun. A ban on handguns, they say, would drastically reduce the rate of violent crime.

We believe that banning handguns won't solve our crime problem. Anyone with an
5 ounce of common sense can see why.

Our Bill of Rights guarantees "the right of the people to keep and bear arms." Government cannot and must not violate this basic freedom under the law. Most of our citizens keep firearms for protection against the small but dangerous minority of armed criminals among us.

10 If we banned handguns, the illegal buying and selling of firearms would become big business overnight on the black market.

Thousands of us already own handguns. A ban would be impractical, if not impossible, to enforce.

And what about the tax increase that would be needed for enforcement? Our city
15 budget is already strained. A new tax would break it.

If someone wants to commit a crime, he will. If he has no handgun, he'll pick up a knife, a pipe, or a bottle. Thieves and murderers are lawbreakers by definition. If they want handguns, no ban is going to stop them. They'll get them on the black market. Or they'll steal them.

20   When only the bad guys have guns, how will the rest of us defend ourselves against assault or robbery? Law-abiding citizens of all ages will be defenseless.

      If the city takes away our handguns, it will be robbing us of our rights. We will be unable to meet our responsibilities to protect ourselves and our loved ones. We emphatically oppose any misguided attempts by the city to compromise our safety and
25   jeopardize our lives.

1. What is the purpose of the editorial?

_____ **(1)** to inform

_____ **(2)** to describe

_____ **(3)** to persuade

2. The third paragraph says banning handguns is unacceptable because

_____ **(1)** other weapons are less effective against crime

_____ **(2)** handgun ownership is guaranteed under the Bill of Rights

_____ **(3)** people will commit crimes regardless of the laws

3. The editorial implies that if handguns were banned, all of the following would happen EXCEPT

_____ **(1)** handguns would be bought and sold illegally

_____ **(2)** taxes would go up

_____ **(3)** the murder rate would drop by half

4. The editorial implies that banning handguns would

_____ **(1)** make it impossible for ordinary people to protect themselves

_____ **(2)** drastically reduce the rate of violent crime

_____ **(3)** solve the crime problem once and for all

ANSWERS ARE ON PAGE 204.

EXERCISE 8

Directions: Now read a second editorial about handguns that has a very different point of view from the last editorial you read. Then put a check in front of the correct answer to the questions that follow.

Three days ago, Lisa Park was murdered. A masked gunman walked into her flower shop and ended her life with a bullet. Less than two weeks before, Officer Donald Smith responded to a domestic disturbance. In a scuffle with an angry husband wielding a handgun, the 31-year-old policeman and father of two was shot dead.

5 Handguns were involved in 22 of the 38 murders here this year. The time has come to ban these weapons.

Americans today are an angry, quick-tempered people in a society that glorifies crime and criminals. A ban on handguns would help redirect our increasingly violent impulses in less lethal directions.

10 More than half of all murders and suicides are committed with handguns. And accidental shootings occur routinely because people who do not know how to use handguns have easy access to them. Firearms training, while certainly recommended, is at best only a partial answer.

Handguns are more lethal than other weapons. There is no defense against them. It
15 doesn't matter how strong you are or how fast. When crimes are committed with knives or other weapons, injury is more common than death. But when crimes are committed with handguns, victims are more likely to die. It's over in an instant. A handgun is small enough to conceal until the last moment, and then it is too late for all the Lisa Parks and Donald Smiths of this world.

20 Handguns have no real value for sport, either. Nobody needs handguns except the police and the armed forces.

What would be the result of a handgun ban? Since Great Britain outlawed handguns in the 1920s, its rate of violent crime has dropped dramatically. Despite the fact that even the British police are unarmed, peace and moderation are the rule in English cities and
25 towns.

We, too, need to ban handguns to make our community a safer place to live and work.

1. What is the main point of the editorial?

_____ **(1)** Handguns are a major cause of violence in the community.

_____ **(2)** Great Britain is an example of effective handgun control.

_____ **(3)** The murder rate in the community is far too high.

2. The word *scuffle* (line 3) means

_____ **(1)** fight

_____ **(2)** race

_____ **(3)** dispute

3. According to the editorial, if a handgun ban went into effect

_____ **(1)** criminals would find it easier to prey on defenseless citizens

_____ **(2)** violent crime would decrease

_____ **(3)** criminals would have all the guns

4. Both editorials about handguns agree that better protection is urgently needed for

_____ **(1)** shop owners

_____ **(2)** handgun owners

_____ **(3)** potential victims of crime

ANSWERS ARE ON PAGE 204.

WRITING ACTIVITY 4

In 1994, an American teenager living in Singapore was arrested on vandalism charges for spray-painting cars. Under Singapore law, vandalism is punishable by caning. The American youth received four painful lashes with a rattan cane. The caning provoked a huge controversy in the United States. Are you for or against such punishment? Write a two- or three-paragraph editorial defending your opinion. In each paragraph, discuss one reason for your position.

ANSWERS WILL VARY.

≡ PRE-GED Practice ≡
EXERCISE 9

Questions 1–3 refer to the following passage.

Is Nuclear Power Safe?

The Dwight Nuclear Power Station opened yesterday in Yerba Valley. The dedication ceremonies were attended by a mixed crowd, including a group of
5 antinuclear protesters.

Owned and operated by Consolidated Electric Company, the Dwight Station is the first of three nuclear plants to be built in the Yerba
10 Valley. The station will serve more than one million customers and at full capacity will generate almost three million kilowatts of electricity.

Situated on 500 acres, the
15 station consists of two reactors, two cooling towers, and two turbine generators. The cost of the entire project has been estimated at more than one billion dollars.

20 Stanley Novak, president of Consolidated Electric, started the festivities promptly at 9:00 A.M. Standing in the control room, he activated the reactors. He then made
25 his way to the entrance, where he addressed the crowd. He told them that the station will save customers money because nuclear power requires less

energy than fossil fuel. He said that the
30 Nuclear Regulatory Commission had certified plant operations as safe.

Novak's remarks were interrupted several times by shouts of protest but drew general applause at the end.

35 Citizens for a Safe Society (CSS), a protest group, displayed signs against nuclear power. CSS spokesman Bill Kerby demanded written assurances from Consolidated Electric that it would
40 follow all recommended safeguards in disposing of nuclear wastes. He also called for a meeting with Novak to discuss radiation hazards.

1. What is the best expanded title for this selection?
   (1) Stanley Novak Speaks About Energy
   (2) Nuclear Plant Opens to Mixed Reaction
   (3) The Dangers of Nuclear Waste
   (4) Nuclear Station to Cut Costs of Electricity
   (5) New Construction in Yerba Valley

2. This passage most likely appeared in
   (1) a scientific journal
   (2) an encyclopedia
   (3) a periodical
   (4) a news story
   (5) an editorial

3. What is the main concern of CSS?
   (1) the acreage of Dwight Station
   (2) the dollar cost of electricity
   (3) the disposal of nuclear waste
   (4) design flaws in the reactors
   (5) the economy of Yerba Valley

Questions 4–7 refer to the following passage.

The medium, or process, of our time—electric technology–is reshaping and restructuring patterns of social interdependence and every aspect of
5 our personal life. It is forcing us to reconsider and reevaluate practically every thought, every action, and every institution formerly taken for granted. Everything is changing—you, your
10 family, your neighborhood, your education, your job, your government, your relation to "the others." And they're changing dramatically.

Societies have always been
15 shaped more by the nature of the media by which men communicate than by the content of the communication. The alphabet, for instance, is a technology that is absorbed by the very
20 young child in a completely unconscious manner, or by osmosis. . . .Words and the meaning of words predispose [incline] the child to think and act automatically in certain ways.
25 The alphabet and print technology fostered and encouraged a fragmenting process, a process of specialism and of detachment. Electric technology fosters and encourages unification and
30 involvement. It is impossible to understand social and cultural changes without a knowledge of the workings of media.

The older training of observation
35 has become quite irrelevant in this new time, because it is based on psychological responses and concepts conditioned by the former technology—mechanization.

—Excerpted from *The Medium Is the Message*, by Marshall McLuhan and Quentin Fiore

4. The main idea of this passage is that
   (1) technology causes division in society
   (2) technology changes our social relationships and personal lives
   (3) society today is confused by technology
   (4) the alphabet is a technology absorbed by young children
   (5) people are unaware how technology is shaping the future

5. The words *by osmosis* (line 21) refer to
   (1) thought
   (2) imagination
   (3) studying hard
   (4) unconscious learning
   (5) a technological event

6. Which of the following best illustrates electric technology?
   (1) newspapers
   (2) conversation
   (3) television
   (4) books
   (5) the alphabet

7. From the last paragraph, you can infer that
   (1) people cannot adjust to new technology
   (2) our past training will help us learn today's skills
   (3) technology will bring people together
   (4) new technology will anger and confuse many people
   (5) we must learn new ways of relating to modern technology

Questions 8–10 refer to the following passage.

Skilled miners from Cornwall, England, began arriving in southwest Wisconsin by the mid-1830s. They brought with them a specialized
5 knowledge of mining gleaned from centuries of deep copper and tin mining in Cornwall.

The new arrivals noticed that the Wisconsin miners worked mainly
10 surface deposits in shallow pits. The Cornish men showed them some better methods. As a result, not only were abandoned mines reopened and expanded, but new ones were
15 discovered. By 1840, Wisconsin was producing more than half of the nation's lead. More settlers poured into the territory. But when the California gold rush began in 1848, the lure of striking
20 it rich became a stronger drawing card.

Many forty-niners who lit out to California in search of gold eventually returned to Wisconsin. Transient miners traveled the state, taking work in the
25 mines wherever they could find it.

Although the mining industry in southwest Wisconsin has a long history, the work was never steady. Whenever market prices dropped, mines shut
30 down, leaving hundreds of men out of work and unsure when or if they would be called back. Some of them managed to survive during these shutdowns by relying on a second occupation—
35 farming.

—Excerpted from "Mining Part of Early History," *Uplands*

8. The Cornish miners
   (1) helped improve mining methods in Wisconsin
   (2) came from Cornwall, California
   (3) helped bring down the price of lead
   (4) worked mainly surface deposits in shallow pits
   (5) were more interested in gold than in lead

9. Which of the following would be the best title for this passage?
   (1) A Short History of Mining in Southwest Wisconsin
   (2) Cornish Miners Settle in Wisconsin
   (3) The California Gold Rush
   (4) Unemployment in the Lead-Mining Industry
   (5) Farming and Mining in Southwest Wisconsin

10. Mining jobs in Wisconsin were lost when
    (1) the California gold rush started
    (2) new iron and copper mines opened in Upper Michigan
    (3) market prices dropped
    (4) the Cornish miners arrived
    (5) settlers poured into the state

Questions 11–13 refer to the following passage.

Today, as a community, we pause to remember two of our own. Lavinia Phelps and Walter Kinski will not soon be forgotten.

5 It was just one year ago today that Lavinia and Walter presided at the official opening of the Y.E.S. (Youth Encounter Seniors) Center here. It was their dream, a place where young and
10 old could share their lives. We are glad that they lived to see it come true and grateful that it lives on, so vibrant, after them.

As many of you know, Lavinia
15 hardly fit the stereotype of the frail old lady in a rocking chair. Dynamic and determined, she worked tirelessly for our needy youth and senior citizens. We remember with admiration and gratitude
20 how she pried investment dollars out of our businesses, churches, public agencies, and even newspapers for the revitalization [bringing to life] of our now-beautiful downtown

25 It was while working on her downtown project that Lavinia met Walter, a retired engineer. Something clicked. They fell in love—with an idea. They decided to help the two neediest
30 groups downtown—aimless youth and lonely (and sometimes frightened) senior citizens. Their radical plan was to help these two groups help each other.

Every day at the Y.E.S. Center you
35 can see young and old doing just that. You'd be surprised how much they have in common and how much each group has to offer the other. Retired nurses show teenage mothers how to take
40 care of their babies. Computer-wise teens show retirees that high tech is nothing to be afraid of and can even be a lot of fun. Troubled and confused youth have sympathetic seniors to turn
45 to for advice. Seniors have strong, healthy new friends whose energy is contagious and whose mere presence reassures them.

You can see them all at the center
50 every day, talking, walking, playing cards, strumming guitars, building furniture, and generally carrying on together across the generations. What a sight! What good news! Walter and
55 Lavinia, thank you.

11. The purpose of this passage is to

(1) persuade
(2) inform
(3) honor
(4) criticize
(5) define

12. Lavinia and Walter were alike in that they

(1) were wealthy
(2) lived in the same neighborhood
(3) were outgoing and talkative
(4) had engineering backgrounds
(5) shared the same vision

13. The word *stereotype* (line 15) means

(1) common image
(2) best example
(3) opposite
(4) personality
(5) temperament

Questions 14–19 refer to the following passage.

To kick off her campaign for re-election, Representative Margaret Palmer took a whirlwind tour of the Southern farming region today.

5 Her first stop was the Spring Agriculture Convention in Torrence, where she spoke briefly to a crowd of about a thousand farmers and agribusinessmen.

10 In her bright pink Chanel suit, jangling bangle bracelets, and broad-brimmed hat festooned with ribbons, Palmer was at the center of attention wherever she went. She was
15 wooing the farm vote in a district where it is hard to find a farmer who has not had to borrow heavily just to hold on to his land.

Palmer worked the crowd with her
20 trademark energy. She laughed easily with conventiongoers who crowded around her. When asked what she intended to do about the farm problem here, she airily promised to seek more
25 federal aid to agriculture.

Later in the day, Palmer toured the 4,000-acre Powell farm. Tramping gamely through the cow barns in her high heels, she stopped frequently to
30 pose for photographers.

"We did not get to talk to her or even to meet her," said Ed Powell, whose grandfather started the farm with just 40 acres more than half a century
35 ago.

The last stop on Palmer's tour was Green Corners, where the political representative urged a gathering of surprised picnickers to remember the importance of homegrown food to the economy. Then she got into her black limousine. Waving from the window, she promised to return again soon.

14. The passage is biased against
    (1) Congress
    (2) Representative Palmer
    (3) designer clothing
    (4) farmers
    (5) agribusiness interests

15. The writer's attitude toward the farmers is best described as
    (1) indifferent
    (2) sympathetic
    (3) impatient
    (4) disdainful
    (5) fearful

16. Representative Palmer's conduct throughout her tour shows that her main concern is

  (1) high fashion
  (2) farmers' problems
  (3) the Powell family
  (4) federal aid to agriculture
  (5) re-election

17. The term *festooned* (line 12) means

  (1) carved
  (2) molded
  (3) decorated
  (4) obtained
  (5) enjoyed

18. Palmer's first stop on the tour was at a

  (1) large farm
  (2) convention
  (3) cow barn
  (4) picnic
  (5) clothing store

19. Which of the following did Palmer promise to the people on her tour?

  (1) more frequent conventions
  (2) better loan programs
  (3) more funding for agriculture
  (4) more contact with voters
  (5) improvements in the economy

ANSWERS ARE ON PAGE 204.

5  Prose Fiction

Novels and short stories are two types of ***prose fiction.*** They both deal with imaginary characters and events. In this section, you will study six basic elements of fiction: setting, plot, character, point of view, literal and figurative language, and theme.

SETTING

The ***setting*** of a story is a combination of place, time, and atmosphere. It tells where and when a story takes place. A story may be set in a real or an imaginary place. It may be also set in the past, present, or future.

PLACE

Place refers to physical setting. A turn-of-the-century castle, a high-rise apartment building, an ocean liner, somebody's living room—these are all examples of place.

The action of a story can be confined to one place, or it can move around from one place to the next. *Jaws* takes place in a small resort community on Long Island. In *The Adventures of Huckleberry Finn*, the action follows the Mississippi River through three states—Missouri, Illinois, and Mississippi. Occasionally, you must infer the physical setting of a story from details the author provides.

Fiction writer Stephen King, shown at left, is well-known for the haunting horror stories he writes. Many of his books have been portrayed on film.

As you read the following paragraph, try to picture the place the author is describing. Then put a check in front of the correct answer to the questions that follow.

> The bright sun overhead warmed the crowds scurrying across the streets and sidewalks. Office workers poured out of modern skyscrapers in unending streams. Cars, cabs, and buses honked and bellowed at each other like angry bulls. Near every street corner, red tulips nodded under budding trees. People scurried in and out of busy restaurants.

1. This scene takes place in a

_____ **(1)** company's headquarters

_____ **(2)** major urban business district

_____ **(3)** restaurant

2. Where does most of the action in this passage take place?

_____ **(1)** in cars, cabs, and buses

_____ **(2)** on city streets and sidewalks

_____ **(3)** in restaurants

For the first question, choice (2), a *major urban business district,* is correct. You can tell from the references to skyscrapers, cars, cabs, buses, and the large numbers of people. For the second question, choice (2), *on city streets and sidewalks,* is correct. Crowds fill the sidewalks and traffic jams the streets.

TIME

The second element of setting is ***time***. Every story takes place in time—in the past, the present, or the future.

Some stories are set in a particular time period. Herman Wouk's *The Winds of War* takes place at the start of World War II. Charles Dickens' *Oliver Twist* is set in mid-19th-century London.

How long a period can a story cover? James Joyce's *Ulysses,* which runs hundreds of pages, covers only one day in 1904. *Roots,* the popular historical novel about slavery by Alex Haley (made into a very moving television miniseries in 1977), plays out over centuries.

Based on the passage on page 90, put a check in front of the correct answer to the questions that follow.

1. When does the scene occur?

_____ **(1)** early morning

_____ **(2)** noon

_____ **(3)** late afternoon

_____ **(4)** evening

2. The scene most probably takes place in

_____ **(1)** May

_____ **(2)** July

_____ **(3)** September

_____ **(4)** December

For the first question, the correct answer is choice (2), *noon*. You can figure this out from the references to the overhead sun and to what is obviously the lunchtime crowd. The correct answer to the second question is choice (1), *May*. You can infer the spring season from the tulips and budding trees. May is the only spring month given in the choices.

ATMOSPHERE

Atmosphere refers to the nonphysical environment of a story, the mood or general feeling in which a story is rooted.

The atmosphere of *The Wizard of Oz,* like the land of Oz itself and the yellow brick road, is bright, colorful, and happy. If you have read Stephen King's *Carrie,* you know that the atmosphere in that high school gym is unbearably tense. The dark, barren, and lonely landscape of Transylvania adds to the already gloomy atmosphere of *Dracula.*

Whenever you read fiction, pay attention to the atmosphere. Notice how it affects the characters and how the characters react to it.

Pay particular attention to the setting and atmosphere in the passage below. Then put a check in front of the correct answers.

The deserted road suddenly gave way to a long, wide boulevard. On either side stood a single row of stately oak trees. The overarching branches formed a protective canopy. From the lower limbs, strands of Spanish moss seemed to wave a gray salute.

5 Tyrone's heart beat faster as the wagon wheels rolled nearer Brentwood. Before the sun dipped beneath the horizon, he had been able to catch a glimpse of the plantation house with its white pillars and the wrought-iron balcony. By some miracle, it was still standing. Four years of civil war had not changed the beautiful old place.

10 But where was Julia? It wouldn't be homecoming until, from the balcony railing, her voice rang out, calling his name. He walked faster, heading hopefully toward the sound of home.

1. The atmosphere of this passage is one of

_____ **(1)** fear

_____ **(2)** hope

_____ **(3)** sadness

2. When he sees that his old home still stands, Tyrone feels

_____ **(1)** doubt

_____ **(2)** disappointment

_____ **(3)** anticipation

3. Where does this scene most likely take place?

_____ **(1)** Oregon

_____ **(2)** Hawaii

_____ **(3)** Louisiana

4. When does the action take place?

_____ **(1)** just before sunrise

_____ **(2)** in the morning

_____ **(3)** late afternoon

For the first question, choice (2), *hope,* is the correct answer. With every step he draws nearer home, Tyrone feels encouraged. The tall trees protect him. The moss seems to salute him. His old home still stands. For the second question, choice (3), *anticipation,* is the correct answer. Tyrone anticipates his reunion with Julia. For the third question, choice (3), *Louisiana,* is the correct answer. The references to Spanish moss, the plantation house, and a recent civil war suggest a Southern setting such as Louisiana. For the fourth question, choice (3), *late afternoon*, is the correct answer. Tyrone catches a glimpse of the house before the sun sets.

EXERCISE 1

Directions: Read the following passage and then put a check in front of the correct answer to the questions that follow.

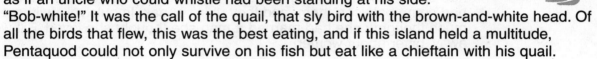

Knowing that there would be ample food, if he could but catch it, Pentaquod pulled his canoe farther inland, hiding it among the oaks and maples which lined the shore, for he knew that he must explore this island quickly. And as he
5   moved among the trees and came to a meadow, he heard the comforting cry so familiar in his days along the great river: "Bob-white! Bob-white!" Now the call came from his left, then from a clump of grass to his right, and sometimes from a spot almost under his feet, but always it was as clear and distinct
10 as if an uncle who could whistle had been standing at his side. "Bob-white!" It was the call of the quail, that sly bird with the brown-and-white head. Of all the birds that flew, this was the best eating, and if this island held a multitude, Pentaquod could not only survive on his fish but eat like a chieftain with his quail.

With extreme caution he started inland, noticing everything, aware that his life
15 might depend upon the carefulness of his observation. With every step he found only reassurance and never a sight of danger: nut trees laden with midsummer shells not yet ripe; droppings of rabbits, and the signs that foxes lived here, and the location of brambled berry bushes, and the woody nests of eagles, and the honeysuckle twisting among the lower branches of the cedar trees.

—Excerpted from *Chesapeake*, by James A. Michener

1. Pentaquod is exploring

_____ **(1)** a forest

_____ **(2)** a river

_____ **(3)** an island

2. The passage most likely takes place during

_____ **(1)** March

_____ **(2)** May

_____ **(3)** July

3. You can infer that Pentaquod is

_____ **(1)** an Indian

_____ **(2)** a bob-white

_____ **(3)** running from someone

4. The atmosphere conveyed by the passage is best described as

_____ **(1)** hopeful

_____ **(2)** tropical

_____ **(3)** lonely

5. The word *ample* (line 1) means

_____ **(1)** cooked

_____ **(2)** more than enough

_____ **(3)** not nearly sufficient

ANSWERS ARE ON PAGE 205.

PLOT

    Plot consists of the action or series of events around which a story is built. Plot tells what happens. An effective plot keeps the reader eager to find out what happens next.

    As you read the following story, pay particular attention to the series of events that contribute to the plot. Then answer the questions that follow.

Early Autumn

    When Bill was very young, they had been in love. Many nights they had spent walking, talking together. Then something not very important had come between them, and they didn't speak. Impulsively [without much thought], she had married a man she thought she loved. Bill went

5   away, bitter about women.

    Yesterday, walking across Washington Square [a park in New York City], she saw him for the first time in years.

    "Bill Walker," she said.

    He stopped. At first he did not recognize her, to him she looked so

10   old.

    "Mary! Where did you come from?"

    Unconsciously [without thinking], she lifted her face as though wanting a kiss, but he held out his hand. She took it.

    "I live in New York now," she said.

15   "Oh"—smiling politely. Then a little frown came quickly between his eyes.

    "Always wondered what happened to you, Bill."

    "I'm a lawyer. Nice firm, way downtown."

    "Married yet?"

20   "Sure. Two kids."

    "Oh," she said.

    A great many people went past them through the park. People they didn't know. It was late afternoon. Nearly sunset. Cold.

    "And your husband?" he asked her.

25   "We have three children. I work in the bursar's [treasurer's] office at Columbia [University]."

"You're looking very . . ." (he wanted to say *old*) ". . . well," he said.

She understood. Under the trees in Washington Square, she found herself desperately reaching back into the past. She had been older than he in Ohio. Now she was not young at all. Bill was still young.

"We live on Central Park West," she said. "Come and see us sometime."

"Sure," he replied. "You and your husband must have dinner with my family some night. Any night. Lucille and I'd love to have you."

The leaves fell slowly from the trees in the square. Fell without wind. Autumn dusk. She felt a little sick.

"We'd love it," she answered.

"You ought to see my kids." He grinned.

Suddenly the lights came on up the whole length of Fifth Avenue, chains of misty brilliance in the blue air.

"There's my bus," she said.

He held out his hand, "Good-bye."

"When . . ." she wanted to say, but the bus was ready to pull off. The lights on the avenue blurred, twinkled, blurred. And she was afraid to open her mouth as she entered the bus. Afraid it would be impossible to utter a word.

Suddenly she shrieked very loudly, "Good-bye!" But the bus door had closed.

The bus started. People came between them outside, people crossing the street, people they didn't know. Space and people. She lost sight of Bill. Then she remembered she had forgotten to give him her address—or to ask him for his—or tell him that her youngest boy was named Bill, too.

—Excerpted from *Something in Common*, by Langston Hughes

1. Bill and Mary broke up because they

_____ **(1)** had very different interests

_____ **(2)** didn't really love each other

_____ **(3)** had a fight about something unimportant

2. After her breakup with Bill, Mary married

____ **(1)** happily and had four children

____ **(2)** a man she thought she loved and had three children

____ **(3)** a lawyer like Bill and named her son after Bill

3. Bill stopped in midsentence when he started to tell Mary how she looked because he thought she looked

____ **(1)** more beautiful

____ **(2)** older

____ **(3)** much heavier

The answer to the first question is choice (3), *had a fight about something unimportant.* You learn this fact in the first paragraph of the story. The answer to the second question is choice (2), *a man she thought she loved and had three children.* In the first paragraph, you learn that "impulsively, she [Mary] had married a man she thought she loved." Line 25 tells you that Mary has three children. The answer to the third question is choice (2), *older.* You learn this in lines 9–10 and again in an aside at the story's midpoint (line 27). The information is set off in parentheses.

CONFLICT

Every event in a story is essential to the plot. Each development advances the action of the story. **Conflict** is the struggle between opposing forces. The points of tension in a story are part of the conflict. There is almost no limit to the forms conflict can take. The conflict can take place within a person, with others, against nations, or against nature. Another common conflict pits good against evil. A single character often wrestles with a difficult decision or struggles to carry on in spite of great pain or intense emotion. Note the chart shown below.

FOUR MAJOR TYPES OF CONFLICT

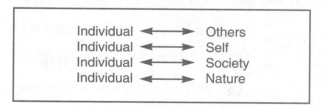

Individual ◄───► Others
Individual ◄───► Self
Individual ◄───► Society
Individual ◄───► Nature

In "Early Autumn," several events precede the **climax,** or turning point, in the story. Bill and Mary had been in love years before. Bill is younger than Mary. They broke up over something unimportant. Mary married another man she thought she loved. Bill became bitter about women. Then, unexpectedly, they meet on a cold afternoon in a park in New York City. Mary is surprised to see Bill. He is amazed at how much older she looks. Mary expects a kiss, but Bill just shakes her hand. They realize they both now live in New York City and that each is married and has children.

At the turning point (climax) of the story, Bill says to Mary, "You're looking very . . ." and his voice trails off. He wants to say "old," and Mary understands what he is thinking. She wants desperately to reach back into the past and make a connection with Bill once again, but with his unfinished sentence she realizes that this isn't possible. Bill invites Mary to bring her family for dinner sometime. She agrees but feels sick inside. Suddenly she sees her bus coming. Bill holds out his hand and says good-bye. Mary is so filled with emotion that she can't speak. She is not able to say good-bye until after the bus door closes, and then she does so in a loud shriek. It dawns on her that they forgot to exchange addresses and that she didn't tell Bill that she has named her son after him.

You can visualize the plot of a story in the general shape of a hill or ocean wave. One or usually several events lead upward toward the climax, or turning point. Once the climax is reached, the plot heads downward toward a **resolution**, or ending.

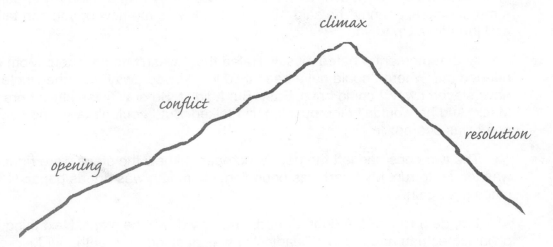

In "Early Autumn," the climax occurs when Bill begins to tell Mary how she looks but doesn't complete the sentence. Mary knows at that point that there is no further connection between her and Bill. From its opening, the story builds toward this moment. Once it is over, the tension is broken and the story ends.

EXERCISE 2

Directions: Read the selection below and then put a check in front of the correct answer to the questions that follow.

"Well, which is it, son?"

"I told you I don't have nothin' to say to you, man. And I ain't your son."

"You're either an Overlord or an East King," Detective Mack said, for about the tenth time. "We know you're one or the other."

5   "Brilliant," I said. The Overlords and the East Kings were the only two gangs in the whole East End.

He ignored the sarcasm, deciding instead to pretend like he already knew everything else there was to know about me. "You're Mary Lucy's boy, Johnny. You live in the Roberts Homes, Building 7, second floor, with your mom and two little sisters. They depend on

10   you. So do yourself a big favor now and level with me. Which of these guys can you identify?" He spread the photographs out on the table.

I didn't like him talking about Mom and the girls. I didn't like being pushed.

Just then, two cops came to the door. They said something to Mack. By the looks on their faces, I knew Eddie was dead. I listened as hard as I could.

15   "Multiple stab wounds," somebody said.

Eddie was my best friend in the world.

Mack walked back over to me. He threw a beefy arm around my shoulder. "We got us a murder case, Johnny," he said. "So you can talk to me now or you can talk to the judge and jury later. Up to you."

20   At that moment, I hated myself. Hated that I wasn't home where Mom and the girls needed me, where I could have been if I'd just stayed away from the whole thing. I could have stayed away. I could have. Easy. But I didn't. So now I was stuck here with this fat Mack. And he wouldn't stop pushing till I talked. But I couldn't talk. And I couldn't let him see I was scared.

25   The two cops had left the door wide open. I knew the steps were right outside. Mack was too fat to run. My heart was pounding. My mouth was dry as paper. Nobody'd ever catch me again.

I made a run for the door, turned, and flew down the steps. Next thing I knew, a plainclothesman had me in a headlock. I was gasping for breath, but I kicked and yelled

30   with all my might.

"Quiet," somebody thundered, and it wasn't the guy who had me. It was somebody new in the stairwell, somebody with the biggest, meanest voice I ever heard. She wore a badge and was tapping a nightstick across her palm.

"Quiet," she said again. "And I mean this minute. Next minute'll be too late."

1. How does Johnny feel about Detective Mack?

_____ **(1)** scared

_____ **(2)** indifferent

_____ **(3)** hostile

2. The conflict in the paragraph beginning "At that moment . . ." is between Johnny and

_____ **(1)** himself

_____ **(2)** the police

_____ **(3)** Eddie

3. The turning point of the action occurs when

_____ **(1)** Johnny encounters the plainclothesman

_____ **(2)** Johnny learns that Eddie is dead

_____ **(3)** the policewoman silences Johnny

4. It can be inferred that this scene takes place in a

_____ **(1)** police station

_____ **(2)** housing project

_____ **(3)** prison

5. Why was Detective Mack questioning Johnny?

_____ **(1)** Johnny was suspected of stabbing Eddie.

_____ **(2)** Johnny had witnessed a stabbing.

_____ **(3)** Mary Lucy had turned her son in to the authorities.

ANSWERS ARE ON PAGE 205.

EXERCISE 3

Directions: Read the selection below and then put a check in front of the correct answer to the questions that follow.

Someone thrust a mask at the young man near Gwen, who had been wounded. Though swaying, and scarcely aware of what was happening, he managed to hold it to his face.

Even so, barely half the passengers were on oxygen at the end of fifteen
5 seconds—the critical time. By then, those not breathing oxygen were lapsing into drowsy stupor; in another fifteen seconds, most were unconscious.

Gwen Meighen received no oxygen, nor immediate help. The unconsciousness, caused by her injuries, deepened.

Then, on the flight deck, Anson Harris, accepting the risk of further structural
10 damage and possible total destruction of the aircraft, made his decision for a high-speed dive, saving Gwen and others from asphyxiation [unconsciousness].

The dive began at twenty-eight thousand feet altitude; it ended, two and a half minutes later, at ten thousand feet.

A human being can survive without oxygen for three to four minutes without damage
15 to the brain.

For the first half of the dive—for a minute and a quarter, down to nineteen thousand feet—the air continued to be rarefied and insufficient to support life. Below that point, increasing amounts of oxygen were present and breathable.

At twelve thousand feet regular breathing was possible. By ten—with little time to
20 spare, but enough—consciousness returned to all aboard Flight Two who had lost it, excepting Gwen. Many were unaware of having been unconscious at all.

—Excerpted from *Airport*, by Arthur Hailey

1. The action in this passage centers around

_____ **(1)** restoring oxygen in the cabin

_____ **(2)** assisting critically injured passengers

_____ **(3)** repairing a damaged aircraft

2. Anson Harris considered a high-speed dive

_____ **(1)** too dangerous to try

_____ **(2)** worth a gamble

_____ **(3)** technically impossible

3. The passengers regained consciousness when the plane

_____ **(1)** dived to 12,000 feet

_____ **(2)** equalized pressure

_____ **(3)** reached 10,000 feet

4. It can be inferred that much oxygen was lost as a result of

_____ **(1)** damage to the aircraft

_____ **(2)** engine malfunction

_____ **(3)** human error

5. The turning point in the action occurred when the

_____ **(1)** passengers regained consciousness

_____ **(2)** pilot decided to dive

_____ **(3)** plane was damaged

ANSWERS ARE ON PAGE 205.

CHARACTER

Character is an essential element of fiction. Writers strive to create characters who are believable and who stir our sympathy. To do this, they often draw upon their own everyday experiences.

Some fictional characters strike us as quite familiar. In Charles Dickens' *A Christmas Carol*, Ebenezer Scrooge reminds us of stingy people we have met in real life. We also recognize Bob Cratchit from our own experiences with people who are good-natured and easygoing.

As you read about fictional characters, think about these three questions:

1. What details does the writer use to describe the characters?

2. What do the characters say and do as they react to others and to different situations?

3. What do the characters' thoughts and feelings reveal about them?

When you study character, it may help you to think of the three questions as sides of a triangle. Each side represents one general category of information about a particular character.

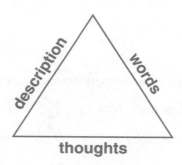

Now let's look at how one distinguished American writer described one of her fictional characters. Read the passage below and then put a check in front of the correct answer to each question.

It was December—a bright frozen day in the early morning. Far out in the country there was an old Negro woman with her head tied in a red rag, coming along a path through the pinewoods. Her name was Phoenix Jackson. She was very old and small and she walked slowly in
5 the dark pine shadows, moving a little from side to side in her steps, with the balanced heaviness and lightness of a pendulum in a grandfather clock. She carried a thin, small cane made from an umbrella, and with this she kept tapping the frozen earth in front of her. This made a grave and persistent noise in the still air that seemed
10 meditative [reflective] like the chirping of a solitary little bird.

She wore a dark striped dress reaching down to her shoe tops, and an equally long apron of bleached sugar sacks, with a full pocket: all neat and tidy, but every time she took a step she might have fallen over her shoelaces, which dragged from her unlaced shoes. She looked
15 straight ahead. Her eyes were blue with age. Her skin had a pattern all its own of numberless branching wrinkles and as though a whole little tree stood in the middle of her forehead, but a golden color ran underneath, and the two knobs of her cheeks were illuminated [lit] by a yellow burning under the dark. Under the red rag her hair came down
20 on her neck in the frailest of ringlets, still black, and with an odor like copper.

—Excerpted from "A Worn Path," by Eudora Welty

1. This passage portrays Phoenix Jackson as

_____ **(1)** old

_____ **(2)** happy

_____ **(3)** confused

2. Phoenix Jackson's clothes are best described as

_____ **(1)** very messy

_____ **(2)** unusual but neat

_____ **(3)** dirty

3. The passage paints Phoenix Jackson as

_____ **(1)** unfriendly

_____ **(2)** stylish

_____ **(3)** odd

The answer to the first question is choice (1), *old.* The passage emphasizes her great age. The writer describes her deep wrinkles and likens her movements to those of a pendulum in a grandfather clock. For question 2, choice (2), *unusual but neat,* is correct. She is described as neat and tidy. Her clothing is simple and a little strange. The answer to the third question is choice (3), *odd.* The old woman's appearance is curious and odd, but in a pleasant sort of way.

Notice how the description of Phoenix Jackson helps reveal her character. We can see her almost perfectly with her red rag turban, tiny stature, slow, rocking gait, aged eyes, many wrinkles, and frail ringlets. Her cane, dress, and dragging shoelaces suggest that she is somewhat odd, or unusual.

EXERCISE 4

Directions: The passage below reveals character through speech and action. As you read it, take note of what the character says and does. Then answer the questions that follow in the space provided.

After a while the fish stopped beating at the wire and started circling slowly again. The old man was gaining line steadily now. But he felt faint again. He lifted some sea water with his left hand and put it on his head. Then he put more on and rubbed the back of his neck.

5   "I have no cramps," he said. "He'll be up soon and I can last. You have to last. Don't even speak of it."

He kneeled against the bow [forward part of a boat] and, for a moment, slipped the line over his back again. I'll rest now while he goes out on the circle and then stand up and work on him when he comes in, he decided.

10   It was a great temptation to rest in the bow and let the fish make one circle by himself without recovering any line. But when the strain showed the fish had turned to come toward the boat, the old man rose to his feet and started the pivoting [turning] and the weaving pulling that brought in all the line he gained.

—Excerpted from *The Old Man and the Sea*, by Ernest Hemingway

1. Why did the old man pour seawater on his head?

_____

2. What do the actions of the old man reveal about his character?

_____

3. To whom is the old man speaking?

_____

4. In this story a *bow* is

_____

ANSWERS ARE ON PAGE 205.

POINT OF VIEW

Character can also be revealed from the first-person point of view. *Point of view* refers to how a particular series of events looks to a specific individual. When two people describe an event that both have witnessed, the descriptions differ because each person speaks from his or her perspective, or viewpoint. Point of view is unique for each person.

When a story is told in the first person, the writer and main character appear to be one and the same. The words *I* and *me* are used frequently as the main character reveals deeply personal thoughts and feelings. The reader has a sense of being able to read the character's mind from the inside.

In the following selection, the writer uses the first-person point of view to help the reader get to know the main character.

EXERCISE 5

Directions: Read the passage below. For each statement that follows, write *A* if the narrator would agree. Write *D* if the narrator would disagree.

The night was not so pleasant as the evening, for it got chilly; and being put between two gentlemen (the rough-faced one and another) to prevent my tumbling off the coach, I was nearly smothered by their falling asleep, and completely blocking me up. They squeezed me so hard sometimes, that I could not help crying out, "Oh, if you
5 please!" which they didn't like at all, because it woke them. Opposite me was an elderly lady in a great fur cloak, who looked in the dark more like a haystack than a lady, she was wrapped up to such a degree. This lady had a basket with her, and she hadn't known what to do with it, for a long time, until she found that, on account of my legs being short, it could go underneath me. It cramped and hurt me so, that it made me perfectly
10 miserable; but if I moved in the least, and made a glass that was in the basket rattle against something else (as it was sure to do), she gave me the cruelest poke with her foot, and said, "Come, don't you fidget. Your bones are young enough, I'm sure!"

—Excerpted from *David Copperfield*, by Charles Dickens

_____ **1.** My ride in the coach was generally comfortable.

_____ **2.** My companions in the coach were friendly.

_____ **3.** I am still growing.

_____ **4.** I am tall for my age.

_____ **5.** The lady treated me in a kindly, reassuring way.

ANSWERS ARE ON PAGE 205.

≡ PRE-GED Practice ≡
EXERCISE 6

Questions 1–7 are based on the passage below, which is written in a Southern dialect.

He was drunk, and weaving about in his saddle; he was over fifty years old, and had a very red face. Everybody yelled at him, and laughed at him, and
5 sassed him, and he sassed back, and said he'd attend to them and lay them out in their regular turns, but he couldn't wait now, because he'd come to town to kill old Colonel Sherburn, and his motto
10 was, "meat first, and spoon vittles to top off on."

He see me, and rode up and says—

"Whar'd you come f'm, boy? You
15 prepared to die?"

Then he rode on. I was scared; but a man says—

"He don't mean nothing; he's always a carryin' on like that, when he's
20 drunk. He's the best-naturedest old fool in Arkansaw—never hurt nobody, drunk nor sober."

Boggs rode up before the biggest store in town and bent his head down
25 so he could see under the curtain of the awning, and yells—

"Come out here, Sherburn! Come out and meet the man you've swindled. You're the houn' I'm after, and I'm a
30 gwyne to have you, too!"

And so he went on, calling Sherburn everything he could lay his tongue to, and the whole street packed with people listening and laughing and
35 going on. By-and-by a proud-looking man about fifty-five—and he was a heap the best dressed man in that town, too—steps out of the store, and the crowd drops back on each side to
40 let him come. He says to Boggs, mighty ca'm and slow—he says:

"I'm tired of this; but I'll endure it till one o'clock. Till one o'clock, mind—no longer. If you open your mouth against
45 me only once, after that time, you can't travel so far but I will find you."

—Excerpted from *The Adventures of Huckleberry Finn,* by Mark Twain

1. From whose point of view is the story told?

(1) Boggs'
(2) Colonel Sherburn's
(3) narrator's
(4) the townspeople's
(5) a store owner's

2. Boggs wants to kill Colonel Sherburn because

   (1) he is jealous of the colonel's wealth
   (2) he thinks Sherburn has cheated him
   (3) Colonel Sherburn insulted Mrs. Boggs
   (4) he is offended by Sherburn's drunken behavior
   (5) Colonel Sherburn started a fight inside a store

3. The narrator describes Colonel Sherburn as

   (1) well dressed
   (2) humble
   (3) grandfatherly
   (4) nervous
   (5) hated by the townspeople

4. How does the narrator feel when Boggs asks him if he is prepared to die (lines 14–15)?

   (1) singled out
   (2) afraid
   (3) amused
   (4) surprised
   (5) angry

5. Colonel Sherburn's final response to Boggs is

   (1) military
   (2) threatening
   (3) drunken
   (4) tolerant
   (5) amused

6. How do the townspeople feel about Boggs?

   (1) They prefer to keep their distance from him.
   (2) They fear him when he's drunk.
   (3) They consider him harmless.
   (4) They think he rides his horse well.
   (5) They are upset by his outbursts.

7. "Whar'd you come f'm, boy?" is an example of

   (1) character
   (2) dialect
   (3) prejudice
   (4) point of view
   (5) setting

ANSWERS ARE ON PAGE 206.

LITERAL AND FIGURATIVE LANGUAGE

In the conversation below, a group of students talk about taking an important test. Joe, Tony, and Sasha use *figurative language* to express their feelings. A figurative expression does not mean exactly what it says. It conveys the speaker's message with words chosen for effect, not literal truth.

JOE: I'm on pins and needles about this test. Aren't you worried, Martha?

MARTHA: Of course not. I've been studying.

TONY: Martha, you're always as cool as a cucumber. But not me. I'm shaking like a leaf. What about you, Sasha?

SASHA: Pins, needles, cucumbers, leaves. I'll tell you one thing—I'm shooting for the stars.

In the example above, Joe is not sitting "on pins and needles." Martha's temperature is not really "as cool as a cucumber." Nor is Sasha really "shooting for the stars."

Now read the same conversation, but written with literal language. With *literal language*, writers say exactly what they mean.

JOE: I'm really nervous about this test. Aren't you worried, Martha?

MARTHA: Not at all. I've been studying.

TONY: You're always calm, Martha. Not me. I'm worried. What about you, Sasha?

SASHA: All I know is I'm aiming for the best grade I can get.

Fiction writers rely on figurative language to express meanings in fresh and surprising ways. Figurative speech, used carefully, catches our attention and holds our interest. Sometimes, it is the most powerful way to show emotion.

Literal: The star burned brightly in the dark sky.

Figurative: The star was a diamond in the black velvet of the sky.

Do you see how the figurative statement is stronger and more expressive? Sometimes an author uses exaggeration for greater effect.

Literal: The old car was sounding worse and worse.

Figurative: The old car coughed and belched. Then it gave a terrible sigh.

The literal meaning, of course, is that the car broke down. But notice how figurative speech can give human qualities to the old machine. A vehicle can't really cough, belch, or sigh, but such language can be much more vivid, or lively.

EXERCISE 7

Directions: Match each figurative expression listed on the left with its literal meaning on the right. Write the correct letter on the line.

Figurative Expressions

_____ **1.** raining cats and dogs

_____ **2.** make hay while the sun shines

_____ **3.** spare the rod and spoil the child

_____ **4.** with hair standing on end

_____ **5.** eat crow

_____ **6.** like death warmed over

_____ **7.** hit the jackpot

_____ **8.** like two peas in a pod

_____ **9.** beat around the bush

_____ **10.** keep your shirt on

Literal Meanings

(a) visibly afraid

(b) sickly in appearance

(c) alike in every way

(d) downpour

(e) give unclear answers

(f) win a lot of money

(g) take advantage of opportunity

(h) discipline children by spanking them

(i) stay calm

(j) admit publicly that you were wrong

ANSWERS ARE ON PAGE 206.

EXERCISE 8

Directions: Write *L* in front of each statement that is used literally. Write *F* in front of each statement that is meant figuratively.

_____ **1.** From the plane, we could see white, fluffy clouds below us.

_____ **2.** To eat the nuts, first crack the shells.

_____ **3.** They'll be jumping for joy when they get the good news.

_____ **4.** Watch your step on the stairway.

_____ **5.** That bucket won't hold water.

_____ **6.** Dogs can be trained to walk on their hind feet.

_____ **7.** The whole world smiled at me.

_____ **8.** It's a marriage made in heaven.

_____ **9.** She was walking on air.

_____ **10.** The children were beside themselves with anticipation.

ANSWERS ARE ON PAGE 206.

EXERCISE 9

Directions: As you read the passage below, notice how figurative language is used. Then put a check in front of the correct answer to the questions that follow.

The tractors came over the roads and into the fields, great crawlers moving like insects, having the incredible strength of insects. They crawled over the ground, laying the track and rolling on it and picking it up. Diesel tractors, puttering while they stood idle; they thundered when they moved, and then settled down to a droning roar. Snubnosed
5   monsters, raising the dust and sticking their snouts into it, straight down the country, across the country, through fences, through dooryards, in and out of gullies [valleys] in straight lines. They did not run on the ground, but on their own roadbeds. They ignored hills and gulches, water courses, fences, houses.

The man sitting in the iron seat did not look like a man; gloved, goggled, rubber dust
10   mask over nose and mouth, he was a part of the monster, a robot in the seat. The thunder of the cylinder sounded through the country, became one with the air and the earth, so that earth and air muttered in sympathetic [shared] vibration. The driver could not control it—straight across country it went, cutting through a dozen farms and straight back.

—Excerpted from *The Grapes of Wrath*, by John Steinbeck

1. The entire first paragraph is a description of

_____ **(1)** monsters

_____ **(2)** tractors

_____ **(3)** insects

2. In the first sentence, the phrase "moving like insects" indicates that the machines

_____ **(1)** flew over the ground

_____ **(2)** kicked up dust

_____ **(3)** crawled across the ground

3. What does the passage imply about the farms?

_____ **(1)** They were being destroyed.

_____ **(2)** Spring planting was in progress.

_____ **(3)** Machinery was being used to increase production.

4. The description of the tractors "raising the dust and sticking their snouts into it" (line 5) is intended to suggest

_____ **(1)** pigs

_____ **(2)** monsters

_____ **(3)** machines

5. The man on the tractor is described as looking like a(n)

_____ **(1)** monster

_____ **(2)** robot

_____ **(3)** insect

ANSWERS ARE ON PAGE 206.

EXERCISE 10

Directions: Read the passage below and then put a check in front of the correct answer to the questions that follow.

One night, a moth flew into the candle, was caught, burnt dry, and held. I must have been staring at the candle, or maybe I looked up when a shadow crossed my page; at any rate, I saw it all. A golden female moth, a biggish one with a two-inch wingspan, flapped into the fire, dropped her abdomen into the wet wax, stuck, flamed, frazzled and
5 fried in a second. Her moving wings ignited like tissue paper, enlarging the circle of light in the clearing and creating out of the darkness the sudden blue sleeves of my sweater, the green leaves of jewelweed by my side, the ragged red trunk of a pine. At once the light contracted again and the moth's wings vanished in a fine, foul smoke. At the same time, her six legs clawed, curled, blackened, and ceased, disappearing utterly. And her
10 head jerked in spasms, making a spattering noise; her antennae crisped and burned away and her heaving mouth parts crackled like pistol fire. When it was all over, her head was, so far as I could determine, gone, gone the long way of her wings and legs. Had she been new, or old? Had she made and laid her eggs, had she done her work? All that was left was the glowing horn shell of her abdomen and thorax [throat]—a fraying, partially
15 collapsed gold tube jammed upright in the candle's round pool.

—Excerpted from *Holy the Firm,* by Annie Dillard

1. The action in this passage centers around

_____ **(1)** the author

_____ **(2)** a fire

_____ **(3)** a moth and a candle

2. "Her moving wings ignited like tissue paper" (line 5) means that the moth's wings

_____ **(1)** were made of tissue paper

_____ **(2)** burned quickly

_____ **(3)** were beautiful

3. The phrase "crackled like pistol fire" (line 11) refers to

_____ **(1)** sights

_____ **(2)** sounds

_____ **(3)** feelings

4. The action in this passage most likely takes place

_____ **(1)** in a forest clearing

_____ **(2)** at a kitchen table

_____ **(3)** on a windowsill

ANSWERS ARE ON PAGE 206.

THEME

The **theme** is the basic idea that underlies a work of fiction and gives it meaning. Rarely, if ever, is it directly stated. You should be able to infer it from the setting, plot, characters, and language. Certain themes appear over and over in literature. Here are some of the most common.

Story	Theme
Huckleberry Finn	The journey from innocence to experience
Robinson Crusoe	Facing and overcoming the unknown
The Wizard of Oz	Good overcomes evil
The Lord of the Flies	Evil overcomes good

There are, of course, many other themes as well. Writers sometimes combine several themes in a single novel or short story. After you read the story below, write its theme on the line provided.

Estara walked carefully between the yawning craters of Novos. Moments before, her bubble rocket had crash-landed on a ridge of soft volcanic sand. Little was left of the vast meteor shower that had carried her off course, hurling the rocket into this strange place.

5   She stared into the black void of space. Somewhere out there was a burning cinder or perhaps a swirl of smoky debris. That was all one would find of the planet Earth. Because of the Great A-War, she and thousands like her had sought a way out of the annihilation [sudden death]. The famous bubble rockets were the answer, but only a few

10 people had been able to secure them. She was sure the rest had perished.

Where were the others, she wondered? Did they reach the earthlike planet Geos, or did they too lose their way?

Ahead of her, Estara saw rocks of many colors, and they glowed.

15 She heard an odd sound like water rushing over rocks. She listened more closely for other sounds. Suddenly, there was a noise like a squeal, perhaps human but possibly an animal. She was not sure. She pulled out her laser gun, stopped, and listened again. Was she safe or was she about to confront an alien? Estara did not know, but she was

20 not going to take any chances.

Which of the themes listed above is also the theme of this passage? You are right if you said that the theme is *facing and overcoming the unknown*. You cannot tell if Estara will overcome whatever awaits her.

EXERCISE 11

Directions: As you read the passage below, note the setting, the plot, and the characters. These will help you identify the theme. Then put a check in front of the correct answer to the questions that follow.

He could just see himself in a new home with a nice back yard, nice trees and lawn, a patio with a barbecue—these things he'd never had, never missed. But why not? A nice garage with a little workshop, like the gringo magazines show all the time. It would be fun.

5 The more he thought about it, the more he liked the idea. What he enjoyed most was the ability he now had—the freedom due to his financial success—that allowed him to make a decision to move where he wanted. This was a luxury little known in his environment. And on the way home from his various out-of-town jobs he began dropping in to look at houses in new tract developments.

It was an old story, but new to Pete. The ghetto protects as well as imprisons. As 10 Pete drove along in the burgeoning [growing] suburbs, he saw tract after tract, with signs advertising the homes for miles in all directions.

> **TWO MINUTES TO PLAZA DEL RIO—
> NOTHING DOWN TO VETS**
> live luxuriously—pay modestly
>
> **TURN RIGHT FOR SUNSET ACRES—
> $200 MOVES YOU IN**
> fireplaces, patios, two-car garages
>
> **LAKETREE HIGHLANDS—
> HOMES TO SUIT YOUR PERSONALITY**
> air conditioning, kitchen built-ins, tile roofs

Pete almost believed it when the salesman at the first office where he stopped told him there were no homes available. He didn't want to argue. But a few days later, when he'd stopped at the fifth or sixth tract office, he was a little better prepared. Not much, but 15 a little.

"No, I'm sorry, Mr. Sandoval. The houses are all taken."

"Well, that one on the corner, it has a for sale sign on it. I want that one."

"It's taken. We haven't had a chance to take the sign down yet."

"I don't believe you. Show me the name of the guy that bought it."

20 "Just a minute," and the salesman went to consult a more experienced man. The other man came back to Pete.

"All our homes are taken," he said simply.

"Then why . . . "

"Make what you want of it, sir, but we have none to sell you."

—Excerpted from *Chicano*, by Richard Vasquez

1. What is Pete doing?

_____ **(1)** mowing his lawn

_____ **(2)** looking for a house

_____ **(3)** shopping for a low-interest mortgage

2. At first, Pete expects that

_____ **(1)** the good houses will be all gone

_____ **(2)** the salesmen will try to sell him anything

_____ **(3)** his money will buy him whatever he wants

3. What is the salesmen's attitude toward Pete?

_____ **(1)** avoidance

_____ **(2)** indifference

_____ **(3)** helpfulness

4. Which of the following statements best expresses the theme of this passage?

_____ **(1)** Everyone dreams about a better life.

_____ **(2)** People do not give up their prejudices without a fight.

_____ **(3)** Financial success is no guarantee against discrimination.

ANSWERS ARE ON PAGE 206.

WRITING ACTIVITY 5

Write three paragraphs about your favorite work of fiction, or choose one you have read in this chapter. In the first paragraph, describe the setting. In the second, summarize the plot. In the third, identify the theme. Refer to the themes listed on page 113 to help you. Be sure to give at least one specific example of how your book's or story's setting, plot, or characterization helps convey the theme.

ANSWERS WILL VARY.

≡ PRE-GED Practice ≡
EXERCISE 12

Questions 1–4 refer to the following passage.

Presently he proceeded again on his forward way. The battle was like the grinding of an immense and terrible machine to him. Its complexities and
5 powers, its grim processes, fascinated him. He must go close and see it produce corpses.

He came to a fence and clambered over it. On the far side, the ground was
10 littered with clothes and guns. A newspaper, folded up, lay in the dirt. A dead soldier was stretched with face hidden in his arm. Farther off there was a group of four or five corpses keeping
15 mournful company. A hot sun had blazed upon the spot.

In this place the youth felt that he was an invader. This forgotten part of the battle ground was owned by the
20 dead men, and he hurried, in the vague apprehension [fear] that one of the swollen forms would rise and tell him to begone.

He came finally to a road from
25 which he could see in the distance dark and agitated bodies of troops, smoke-fringed. In the lane was a blood-stained crowd streaming to the rear. The wounded men were cursing,
30 groaning, and wailing. In the air, always, was a mighty swell of sound that it seemed could sway the earth. With the courageous words of the artillery and the spiteful sentences of the musketry
35 mingled red cheers. And from this region of noises came the steady current of the maimed [wounded].

One of the wounded men had a shoeful of blood. He hopped like a
40 schoolboy in a game. He was laughing hysterically.

One was swearing that he had been shot in the arm through the commanding general's mismanagement
45 of the army. One was marching with an air imitative of some sublime drum major. Upon his features was an unholy mixture of merriment and agony.

—Excerpted from *The Red Badge of Courage,* by Stephen Crane

1. The youth walking among the wounded is portrayed as feeling

    (1) immortal
    (2) optimistic
    (3) neutral
    (4) worried
    (5) like an invader

2. Where does the scene take place?

    (1) in a hospital
    (2) on a battlefield
    (3) in an army camp
    (4) on a troopship
    (5) at a retirement facility

3. When the author says that "the battle was like the grinding of an immense and terrible machine" (lines 2–4), he means that

    (1) machines are terrible
    (2) the war was being fought with many tanks
    (3) soldiers were fighting in large formations
    (4) war is inhuman
    (5) the battle seemed endless

4. Which of the following best states the theme of this passage?

(1) If you are not prepared for battle, you'll be gravely injured.
(2) Victory brings honor and glory.
(3) War brings pain and misery.
(4) One victory doesn't decide a war.
(5) Generals are responsible for the lives of their men.

Questions 5–7 refer to the following passage.

"I have had so many hardships in this life," said Simple, "that it is a wonder I'll live until I die. I was born young, black, voteless, poor, and

5   hungry, in a state where white folks did not even put Negroes on the census. My daddy said he were never counted in his life by the United States government. And nobody could find a

10   birth certificate for me nowhere. It were not until I come to Harlem that one day a census taker dropped around to my house and asked where were I born and why, also my age and if I was still

15   living. I said, 'Yes, I am here, in spite of all.'

" 'All of what?' asked the census taker. 'Give me the data.'

" 'All of my corns and bunions, for

20   one,' I said. 'I were borned with corns. Most colored peoples get corns so young, they must be inherited. As for bunions, they seem to come natural, we stands on our feet so much. These

25   feet of mine have stood in everything from soup lines to the draft board. They have supported everything from a packing trunk to a hongry woman. My feet have walked ten thousand

30   miles running errands for white folks and another ten thousand trying to keep up with colored. My feet have stood before altars, at crap tables, bars, graves, kitchen doors, welfare windows,

35   and social security railings. Be sure and include my feet on that census you are taking,' I told that man.

"Then I went on to tell him how my feet have helped to keep the American

40   shoe industry going, due to the money I have spent on my feet. 'I have wore out seven hundred pairs of shoes, eighty-nine tennis shoes, forty-four summer sandals, and two hundred and

45   two loafers. The socks my feet have bought could build a knitting mill. The razor blades I have used cutting away corns could pay for a razor plant. Oh, my feet have helped to make America

50   rich, and I am still standing on them.' "

—Excerpted from "Census" in
Simple's Uncle Sam, by
Langston Hughes

5. The tone of Simple's speech is best described as

(1) objective
(2) patient
(3) long-suffering
(4) hopeful
(5) arrogant

6. Simple regards his country with

(1) resentment and bitterness
(2) optimism
(3) hatred
(4) affection
(5) loyalty and pride

7. What is the best title for this passage?

(1) The Census Taker
(2) Making a Living on Your Feet
(3) Simple's Corns
(4) The Hardships of Being Black
(5) Wealth and Poverty in America

Questions 8–11 refer to the following passage.

On Sunday, at breakfast, his grandmother asks, "What time did you get in?"

5 He knows that she knows. The light was on in their bedroom when he pulled into the drive; off, as he came up the stairs.

"I don't know. Twelve? Twelve-thirty?"

10 "One-thirty," she says.

"One-thirty, then." He nods amiably [cheerfully], helping himself to the toast she has kept warm for him in the oven. The small breakfast nook is washed in
15 sunlight. Sun glints off the jar of honey sitting on the table, filtering through the pale yellow curtains at the window. His head sings with an intricate, melodic line—Telemann? Marais? John Bull? He
20 cannot remember, but he loves those fresh and unfamiliar instruments, the recorder, the harpsichord; their simple statements of truth. He wonders what the weather is like in Dallas. Sunny, he
25 hopes. Warm.

"How can you expect to get a decent night's sleep, coming in at that hour?" She is frowning across the table at him.

30 "I give up. How can I?"

She sighs. "Everything's a joke with you, isn't it?"

"Grandmother, you know something, I'm nuts about you," he says
35 cheerfully. "You're always agitating. I think it's great. You oughta run for President. No kidding."

He gets to his feet, pushing the chair back.

40 "Where are you going?"

"Outside to wash my car."

"Well, don't get chilled. It's not summer, you know."

"I know, I know!"

—Excerpted from *Ordinary People*, by Judith Guest

8. The action of this passage centers around

   (1) a breakfast conversation
   (2) a shared interest in music
   (3) an election
   (4) washing a car
   (5) health

9. How does the young man behave toward his grandmother?

   (1) rudely
   (2) angrily
   (3) sarcastically
   (4) affectionately
   (5) disrespectfully

10. The woman fusses about her grandson because she is

    (1) a nag
    (2) concerned about his health
    (3) in a bad mood
    (4) lonely
    (5) feeling ill

11. What does the grandson plan to do after breakfast?

    (1) go to a party
    (2) listen to Telemann and Marais
    (3) drive to Dallas
    (4) wash the dishes
    (5) wash the car

Questions 12–14 refer to the following passage.

Yossarian walked out of the office and down the stairs into the dark, tomblike street, passing in the hall the stout woman with warts and two
5   chins, who was already on her way back in. There was no sign of Milo outside. There were no lights in any of the windows. The deserted sidewalk rose steeply and continuously for
10 several blocks. He could see the glare of a broad avenue at the top of the long cobblestone incline. The police station was almost at the bottom; the yellow bulbs at the entrance sizzled in the
15 dampness like wet torches. A frigid, fine rain was falling. He began walking slowly, pushing uphill. Soon he came to a quiet, cozy, inviting restaurant with red velvet drapes in the windows and a
20 blue neon sign near the door that said: TONY'S RESTAURANT, FINE FOOD AND DRINK. KEEP OUT. The words on the blue neon sign surprised him mildly for only an instant. Nothing warped
25 seemed bizarre anymore in his strange, distorted surroundings. The tops of the sheer buildings slanted in weird, surrealistic [unnatural] perspective, and the street seemed tilted. He raised the
30 collar of his warm woolen coat and hugged it around him. The night was raw. A boy in a thin shirt and thin tattered trousers walked out of the darkness on bare feet. The boy had
35 black hair and needed a haircut and shoes and socks. His sickly face was pale and sad. His feet made grisly, soft, sucking sounds in the rain puddles on the wet pavement as he passed, and
40 Yossarian was moved by such intense pity for his poverty that he wanted to smash his pale, sad, sickly face with his fist and knock him out of existence because he brought to mind all the
45 pale, sad, sickly children in Italy that same night who needed haircuts and needed shoes and socks. He made Yossarian think of cripples and of cold and hungry men and women, and of all
50 the dumb, passive, devout mothers with catatonic [expressionless] eyes nursing infants outdoors that same night with chilled animal udders bared insensibly to that same raw rain. Cows. Almost on
55 cue, a nursing mother padded past holding an infant in black rags, and Yossarian wanted to smash her too, because she reminded him of the barefoot boy in the thin shirt and thin,
60 tattered trousers and of all the shivering, stupefying [astounding] misery in a world that never yet had provided enough heat and food and justice for all but an ingenious [clever]
65 and unscrupulous [immoral] handful. What a lousy earth!

—Excerpted from *Catch-22*, by Joseph Heller

12. Heller uses the "frigid, fine rain" (lines 15–16) to
    (1) stand for spiritual cleansing
    (2) suggest the coming of spring
    (3) create a gloomy atmosphere
    (4) show the freshening power of water
    (5) emphasize Yossarian's disagreeable nature

13. The central conflict in this passage is between Yossarian and
    (1) an unjust world
    (2) the restaurant
    (3) the weather
    (4) the boy
    (5) himself

14. The tone of the passage is
    (1) flowery
    (2) informal
    (3) passive
    (4) pessimistic
    (5) violent

ANSWERS ARE ON PAGE 206.

6 Poetry

In this chapter, you will learn what poetry is. You will look at the differences between prose and poetry. You will study a poem's rhyme and rhythm. You will determine the meaning of various poems. And you will look at poetic elements such as imagery, figurative language, and symbolism.

WHAT IS POETRY?

Poetry is an art form that communicates feelings or ideas by use of stanzas, or verses, instead of paragraphs; it uses figurative language; and it has rhythm and, sometimes, rhyme.

Poetry has a distinct form of its own—or the way it looks on a page. The words in a poem are written in lines. Some are short; some are long. Some lines are complete sentences, and others are not. Some lines are indented for special emphasis, or to give the poem visual appeal.

The best way to become acquainted with poetry is to compare it with prose.

In his poem "The Eagle," Alfred, Lord Tennyson depicts the great bird in its natural surroundings.

First read a prose translation of the poem. Then look at the original poem on the next page. What difference do you see between the two?

Prose Translation

The eagle clings to a rocky ledge high in the blue sky. It studies the small waves in the sea below. Suddenly, it dives to the surface of the water.

Maya Angelou, shown at left, is an award-winning writer who has written several books of poetry. The volumes of her autobiography are continuing best-sellers.

Now read the original poem as written by Tennyson.

The Eagle

He clasps the crag with crooked hands
Close to the sun in lonely lands,
Ringed with the azure world, he stands.

The wrinkled sea beneath him crawls;
He watches from his mountain walls
And like a thunderbolt he falls.

Which version captures your interest more—the prose version or the original poem? Notice the familiar structure of the prose translation. It is written in sentences that form a paragraph.

RHYTHM

By contrast, the poem is written in two stanzas of three lines each. Notice the **rhythm** of the poem's stanzas. The rhythm is the sound and the beat of each line and verse. One change in the order or selection of the words would ruin the rhythmic unity of the poem as a whole.

Poetry stirs our senses. Its figurative language speaks to the imagination. "The wrinkled sea beneath him crawls" is a beautiful example of figurative speech that conveys a physical reality more effectively than literal language could. The sea is not wrinkled; it does not crawl. But those words enable us to see it from where the eagle sits.

In the last line of the poem, the poet has chosen exactly the right words and not one more. You can see the dive, hear the wings, and sense the speed. You can almost hear the splash. The words are stunning and hard to forget. This is poetry.

RHYME

Rhyme heightens a poem's effect. In traditional poetry, sounds are repeated at the ends of lines. Rhyme makes poetry easier to remember. Because poetry is meant to be read aloud, rhyme also adds to the enjoyment of it. Rhyming sounds emphasize what the poet wants us to understand. Reread Tennyson's poem "The Eagle." Which words rhyme in each stanza?

You were correct if you identified the rhyming words *hands, lands,* and *stands* in the first stanza and the rhyming words *crawls, walls,* and *falls* in the second stanza.

EXERCISE 1

Directions: Read the poem below and then answer the questions that follow.

A Sad Song About Greenwich Village

She lives in a garret
　　Up a haunted stair,
And even when she's frightened
　　There's nobody to care.

5　　She cooks so small a dinner
　　She dines on the smell,
And even if she's hungry
　　There's nobody to tell.

She sweeps her musty lodging
10　　As the dawn steals near,
And even when she's crying
　　There's nobody to hear.

I haven't seen my neighbor
　　Since a long time ago,
15　　And even if she's dead
　　There's nobody to know.

　　　　　　　　—Frances Park

1. Which words rhyme in each stanza?

Stanza 1: ＿＿＿＿＿＿＿＿＿＿＿＿　　＿＿＿＿＿＿＿＿＿＿＿＿

Stanza 2: ＿＿＿＿＿＿＿＿＿＿＿＿　　＿＿＿＿＿＿＿＿＿＿＿＿

Stanza 3: ＿＿＿＿＿＿＿＿＿＿＿＿　　＿＿＿＿＿＿＿＿＿＿＿＿

Stanza 4: ＿＿＿＿＿＿＿＿＿＿＿＿　　＿＿＿＿＿＿＿＿＿＿＿＿

2. This poem is about a

＿＿＿ **(1)** run-down neighborhood

＿＿＿ **(2)** haunted house in the city

＿＿＿ **(3)** lonely older woman who lives alone

ANSWERS ARE ON PAGE 207.

HOW TO READ POETRY

Before you read a poem, look at its title. Keep it in mind as you read. How does the title relate to the body of the poem?

Remember that, much like a paragraph, each stanza of a poem represents a different thought. Stanzas are also separated by space breaks, much as paragraphs are set off by indents.

Look carefully at how the poem is written. Look at the lines of each stanza. Notice that the first word of a line may be capitalized even if it does not begin a sentence. Don't let this confuse you. Sentences in poetry are indicated by periods. Capital letters don't necessarily mean the start of a new sentence; sometimes they just emphasize the start of a line. If a capital is preceded by a period, you know that it begins a new sentence. If there is no period, the old sentence has not ended.

Study the end of each line. Are there any punctuation marks? There may not be. But if there are, remember that punctuation works the same way in poetry as in prose. If there is no punctuation at the end of a line, simply continue reading without a pause. Let the punctuation tell you when to pause; do not automatically pause at the end of a line.

Look at the following poem by William Carlos Williams.

The Term

A rumpled sheet
of brown paper
about the length

and apparent bulk
5 of a man was
rolling with the

wind slowly over
and over in
the street as

10 a car drove down
upon it and
crushed it to

the ground. Unlike
a man it rose
15 again rolling

with the wind over
and over to be as
it was before.

In this poem, the first sentence does not end until the word *ground* in the fifth stanza.

The second sentence, beginning with "Unlike a man," is read straight through to the end of the poem. In the entire poem, only the first letters of each sentence are capitalized. After the first line, which begins a sentence, every line begins with a lowercase letter.

THE MEANING OF POETRY

Now let's look again at the poem and see what Williams is saying. The title says that this poem is about a term. But if you read it carefully, you will see that a specified length of time is not what is being discussed.

Look at the two statements in the poem. They refer to the term—the span of existence—of a man and of a large crumpled sheet of brown paper roughly the same size and shape (but not weight) of a man. The term of the paper is endless. It is unaffected even after an automobile drives over it. The term of a man would be cut short by such an event.

Even though the poem is short, it provides much to visualize and think about. You can see that huge sheet of paper rolling down the street where the wind is blowing it. You can see the car roll over it and drive on. You can see that the paper keeps right on going, basically unchanged by what just happened to it.

Contrast this with something the approximate shape and size (but not weight) of the paper—a man. A man could never emerge from beneath the wheels of a moving car the same as he was before.

Why does Williams make this comparison? Why has he drawn this simple but serious picture? What do we learn from it? "The Term" has a message about the fragility of life. It compares a living human being to an old ball of paper. The paper has no real value and nothing to fear. Even a moving automobile cannot hurt it. But the living man, whose value is beyond calculation, has much to fear. Life for him is as dangerous as it is precious.

Poetry, like prose, consists of a main idea and the details that enrich it. You can draw inferences from these elements. Beginning with the title, read a new poem straight through. See if you can find the main idea. What does the title tell you? You may need to read a poem several times to figure it out.

EXERCISE 2

Directions: Read the poem below and then put a check in front of the correct answer to the questions that follow.

Taught Me Purple

My mother taught me purple
   Although she never wore it.
Wash-grey was her circle,
   The tenement her orbit.

5   My mother taught me golden
   And held me up to see it,
Above the broken molding,
   Beyond the filthy street.

   My mother reached for beauty
10   And for its lack she died,
Who knew so much of duty
   She could not teach me pride.

—Evelyn Tooley Hunt

1. The poet is expressing feelings of

_____ **(1)** love and sadness

_____ **(2)** bitterness and self-hatred

_____ **(3)** pride and fearlessness

2. The poet says that her mother

_____ **(1)** reached for beauty and found it

_____ **(2)** died for want of beauty

_____ **(3)** inhabited a beautiful world of colors

3. The mother's "circle" was "wash-grey" because she

_____ **(1)** was a laundress

_____ **(2)** was a poor woman living in a gloomy environment

_____ **(3)** had too difficult a life to think about beautiful things

4. The terms *purple* and *golden* refer to

_____ **(1)** colorful clothes the mother wore

_____ **(2)** the brighter side of life

_____ **(3)** beautiful sunsets the mother showed the daughter

5. Explain what the poet meant when she said that her mother "knew so much of duty she could not teach me pride."

_____

_____

_____

6. Which two sets of words rhyme in the third stanza?

_____   _____

_____   _____

ANSWERS ARE ON PAGE 207.

IMAGERY

The word *poet* comes from the Greek word *poesis*, meaning "to make." To create new and exciting language, a poet needs imagination.

Poets use carefully chosen words to create images and figures of speech. The language of a poem enables us to understand the poet's vision almost as if we could experience it with our own senses. Just as an artist uses colors to make a painting, so a poet chooses words to convey thoughts and feelings. Images and figurative language make poetry come alive.

Poets use ***imagery*** to share their way of seeing the world. Images are what the words of a poem enable you to see. They are the pictures that come into your mind as you read the poet's words. They are your link to the poet's imagination.

Read the poem below carefully. Then describe in your own words the images the poem enables you to see.

Cat's World

The white cat steps carefully
almost mechanical
along the crumbling stone wall
then sits still
and sergeant straight.

—Ed Beatty

Lines 1 and 2

_____

_____

Line 3

_____

_____

Line 4

_____

_____

Line 5

_____

_____

Lines 1 and 2 give the image of a white cat walking along so precisely that it resembles a mechanical device, perhaps a windup toy. Line 3 shows that the cat is balancing on an old, broken cement wall. In line 4 the cat stops walking and sits down. Line 5 describes the cat's posture in terms of military straightness, "sergeant straight."

FIGURATIVE LANGUAGE

As you have already learned, figurative language goes beyond the literal meaning of words. Poets use figurative language to heighten the visual and emotional power of their words. In this section, you will study three specific types of figurative language:

- simile and metaphor

- personification

- symbolism

SIMILE AND METAPHOR

A *simile* uses the words *like*, *as*, or *than* to make a comparison. If you say that someone is as "light as a feather," you mean that the person has a very slight figure, not that he or she weighs literally no more than a feather.

A man who says to the woman he loves, "Your eyes are *like* diamonds," is not saying that the woman's eyes look like jewelry but that they shine with brilliance like diamonds do.

The legendary Paul Bunyan is described as being "taller than a mountain." This expression is not meant to give his actual height but to convey Bunyan's giantlike appearance. You can recognize these similes by the use of the words *as, like,* or *than.*

A *metaphor* is a comparison without the use of the words *like, as,* or *than.*

Tate University played with feet of lead in its loss to Kemper.

The feet of the Tate players are compared to lead, which is heavy and lifeless. So the metaphor means that the Tate team played without energy or speed.

EXERCISE 3

Directions: Write *S* in front of the statements that are similes. Write *M* in front of the statements that are metaphors.

_____ **1.** "She walks in beauty, like the night."

_____ **2.** "... time flows on and on,
That narrow noiseless river...."

_____ **3.** She had the strength of a lioness and the cunning of a fox.

_____ **4.** Superman is "faster than a speeding bullet and more powerful than a locomotive."

_____ **5.** "The moon is a balloon."

ANSWERS ARE ON PAGE 207.

PERSONIFICATION

Personification is another type of figurative language. When writers use this technique, they give an object the characteristics of living things or use human qualities to describe something that is not human. Personification helps reveal a poet's vision.

Tennyson's poem "The Eagle" begins with the line "He clasps the crag with crooked hands." Ralph Waldo Emerson once observed, "The wings of time are black and white." What do these lines by Tennyson and Emerson have in common?

Tennyson's eagle has hands; eagles do not really have hands. Emerson describes time as having wings; literally speaking, wings belong only to birds and certain other creatures. Eagles cannot have hands any more than time can have wings, except by means of personification.

EXERCISE 4

Directions: Read the poem below and then answer the questions that follow.

Night

Night gathers itself into a ball of dark yarn.
Night loosens the ball and it spreads.
The lookouts from the shores of Lake Michigan
    find night follows day,
      and ping! ping! across the sheet gray
      the boat lights put their signals.
Night lets the dark yarn unravel,
Night speaks and the yarns change
    to fog and blue strands.

—Carl Sandburg

1. Night is described in line 1 as a

_____

2. In lines 1–7, which four action words are used to personify night?

_____   _____

_____   _____

3. In lines 8 and 9, after night speaks, what two things do the yarns change into?

_____   _____

ANSWERS ARE ON PAGE 207.

SYMBOLISM

A symbol is anything that represents something else. McDonald's yellow arches symbolize the fast-food chain. A wave of the hand is a gesture symbolizing hello or good-bye.

The following poem relies heavily on romantic ***symbolism***. Even the title is symbolic. Since valentines symbolize the heart, they are used to express love. In addition to the valentine and the heart, this poem also uses a third symbol to express the depths of the poet's feelings. What is this third symbol?

Valentines

Forgive me if I have not sent you
a valentine
but I thought you knew
that you already have my heart
Here take the space where my
heart goes
I give that to you too

—Henry Dumas

The heart in the poem symbolizes the poet's feelings of love. But he also says that his beloved already has his heart. Since he cannot give what he has already given, he offers the space that encloses his heart.

That space around the poet's heart is the third symbol in this poem. Here, Dumas uses it to symbolize a greater love than his heart alone represents.

EXERCISE 5

Questions 1–4 are based on the poem below.

Apartment House

A filing-cabinet of human lives
Where people swarm like bees in tunneled hives,
Each to his own cell in the towered comb,
Identical and cramped—we call it home.

—Gerald Raftery

1. What is the main image of this poem?
   (1) bees swarming in a hive
   (2) people happy in their bustling environment
   (3) people locked in a metal file drawer
   (4) a comb constructed of cells
   (5) impersonal, dehumanizing housing

2. The second line in the poem is an example of
   (1) personification
   (2) exaggeration
   (3) simile
   (4) metaphor
   (5) symbolism

3. Two words that rhyme in the poem are
   (1) swarm and bees
   (2) cabinet and cramped
   (3) tunneled and towered
   (4) comb and home
   (5) bees and each

4. The poet describes people's living spaces as being
   (1) spacious and airy
   (2) well lit and in good order
   (3) comfortable and inviting
   (4) crowded and similar
   (5) busy and square-shaped

ANSWERS ARE ON PAGE 208.

PRE-GED Practice
EXERCISE 6

Questions 1–4 are based on the poem below.

Harlem Night Song

Come,
Let us roam the night together
Singing

I love you

5   Across
The Harlem rooftops
Moon is shining.
Night sky is blue
Stars are great drops
10 Of golden dew.

Down the street
A band is playing.

I love you

Come,
15 Let us roam the night together
Singing

—Langston Hughes

1. The poet compares stars to

   (1) golden dewdrops
   (2) a band playing
   (3) the shining moon
   (4) Harlem
   (5) the blue night sky

2. Lines 9 and 10 illustrate

   (1) personification
   (2) simile
   (3) metaphor
   (4) symbolism
   (5) internal rhyme

3. According to the poem, a vital part of Harlem life at night is its

   (1) crowded streets
   (2) honking horns
   (3) music
   (4) warm weather
   (5) moonlight

4. The poet is expressing feelings of

   (1) anger
   (2) sadness
   (3) disappointment
   (4) confusion
   (5) happiness

ANSWERS ARE ON PAGE 208.

UNDERSTANDING POETRY

A poem's rhythm, images, and figurative language will help you understand it. If you already know something about the background of the poet, this will help you, too. If not, you can expect to discover something about the poet as you unlock the meaning of a poem.

EXERCISE 7

Directions: Read the poem below and then put a check in front of the correct answer to the questions that follow.

Crows

Hear them speak like men
to one another. Their gravel voices
are thunder breaking the sky,
a gun cracking air,
5 the bad air
filled with birds whose wings
tip indigo [blue] in the light.

Beneath them, men with blue guns
turn up the whites of their eyes.
10 The feathers,
the feathers come apart, falling
specks of dust.

My ears want to hear them
begin to speak,
15 to hear the dark berries
uncoil through flesh.
They are quiet,
so still
I wait for a breath
20 to escape the warm feathers.

—Linda Hogan

1. Which of the following is an example of metaphor?

_____ **(1)** "their gravel voices are thunder"

_____ **(2)** "men with blue guns turn up the whites of their eyes"

_____ **(3)** "I wait for a breath to escape the warm feathers"

2. Lines 1 and 2 are an example of

_____ **(1)** metaphor

_____ **(2)** internal rhyme

_____ **(3)** simile

ANSWERS ARE ON PAGE 208.

WRITING ACTIVITY 6

Choose one poem from this chapter that you enjoyed and read it aloud. Try to follow it word by word and line by line. Pause where the punctuation tells you to do so. Look up any words that are unfamiliar to you. Notice if ordinary words are used figuratively. Rewrite the poem in your own words. Use ordinary words in place of any figurative or difficult language.

ANSWERS WILL VARY.

PRE-GED Practice

EXERCISE 8

Questions 1–6 refer to the poem below.

The Bus

I was the last passenger of the day,
I was alone on the bus,
I was glad they were spending all that money
just getting me up Eighth Avenue.
5   Driver! I shouted, it's you and me tonight,
let's run away from this big city
to a smaller city more suitable to the heart,
let's drive past the swimming pools of Miami Beach,
you in the driver's seat, me several seats back,
10   but in the racial cities we'll change places
so as to show how well you've done up North,
and let us find ourselves some tiny American fishing village
in unknown Florida
and park right at the edge of the sand,
15   a huge bus pointing out,
metallic, painted, solitary,
with New York plates.

—Leonard Cohen

1. The bus is from
   - **(1)** Miami Beach
   - **(2)** New York City
   - **(3)** Tampa Bay
   - **(4)** a small city
   - **(5)** Chicago

2. The mood of this poem can best be described as one of
   - **(1)** sadness
   - **(2)** confusion
   - **(3)** escapism
   - **(4)** cheerfulness
   - **(5)** boastfulness

3. The passenger and the driver will change places "in the racial cities" because the driver is
   - **(1)** prejudiced
   - **(2)** friendly
   - **(3)** black
   - **(4)** white
   - **(5)** fearful

4. The passenger wants to trade places with the driver because he
   - **(1)** has always wanted to drive a bus
   - **(2)** wants to drive up Eighth Avenue
   - **(3)** wants to collect fares from boarding passengers
   - **(4)** would like to show others that the bus driver has done well
   - **(5)** wants to go swimming in Miami Beach

5. The passenger wants to go
   - **(1)** up North
   - **(2)** to New York
   - **(3)** to Miami Beach
   - **(4)** up Eighth Avenue
   - **(5)** to a small city in Florida

6. What is the main idea of this poem?
   - **(1)** escaping from big city life
   - **(2)** the American landscape
   - **(3)** the loneliness of riding the bus at night
   - **(4)** the great wealth of Miami Beach
   - **(5)** integrating public transportation

Questions 7–10 refer to the poem below.

Voice

At school my voice is a plain
the soil of northern terrain
a great field of monotone days
flatland from October to May.

At home it is a row of hills
a southern sierra regaining color
or a Mexican range come every summer
my voice from June to September.

—Gabriel Olvera

7. The tone of this poem can best be described as
   (1) serious
   (2) fearful
   (3) bitter
   (4) depressing
   (5) youthful

8. Which statement is true?
   (1) The first four lines are all similes.
   (2) Every line except the last is a metaphor.
   (3) The last line illustrates humor.
   (4) The title illustrates personification.
   (5) The word *school* is used metaphorically.

9. What is the poet comparing?
   (1) himself in two environments
   (2) speech and silence
   (3) the seasons
   (4) plains and hills
   (5) Mexico and the United States

10. When is the poet happiest?
    (1) when he is at school
    (2) in the fall
    (3) in summer
    (4) in winter
    (5) when his voice is a plain

Questions 11–14 refer to the poem below.

I Ask My Mother to Sing

She begins, and my grandmother joins her.
Mother and daughter sing like young girls.
If my father were alive, he would play
his accordion and sway like a boat.

5 I've never been in Peking, or the Summer Palace,
nor stood on the great Stone Boat to watch
the rain begin on Kuen Ming Lake, the picnickers
running away in the grass.

But I love to hear it sung;
10 how the waterlilies fill with rain until
they overturn, spilling water into water,
then rock back, and fill with more.

Both women have begun to cry.
But neither stops her song.

—Li-Young Lee

11. The phrases "sing like young girls" and "sway like a boat" are examples of

(1) simile
(2) metaphor
(3) exaggeration
(4) personification
(5) symbolism

12. You can infer that the song is about

(1) young girls
(2) a man playing an accordion
(3) mothers and daughters
(4) beautiful places in China
(5) great sadness

13. Who is "daughter" (line 2)?

(1) the poet
(2) the poet's daughter
(3) the poet's mother
(4) the poet's grandmother
(5) a picnicker at Kuen Ming Lake

14. How does the poet feel as she hears the song?

(1) angry
(2) embarrassed
(3) pleased
(4) bitter
(5) confused

ANSWERS ARE ON PAGE 208.

7 Drama

What separates drama from other types of literature? **Drama** is written to be performed. Dramatists, or playwrights, write their stories in the form of dialogue for actors to speak aloud onstage. The best place to appreciate drama is in a theater. There you can watch and listen as actors bring their characters to life. You can see every detail of the physical setting.

Dramatic works generally take one of three forms: comedy, tragedy, or social drama. **Comedy** takes a light approach toward its subject, although the subject itself may be serious. Generally, comedies have happy endings. The dialogue tends to be funny or satirical, evoking recognition and laughter.

Tragedy tells the story of a character who comes to ruin as the result of a flaw in his nature or forces beyond his control. **Social drama** deals with familiar problems in true-to-life situations. Arthur Miller's *Death of a Salesman,* the story of the emotional disintegration [breakdown] of an ordinary working man, is one of the best-known social dramas of all time.

THE ELEMENTS OF DRAMA

Every drama is built upon the same basic elements:

- stage directions and punctuation
- dialogue
- character
- action
- idea

As you read the following scene, look for the basic elements. The **stage directions** appear in *italic* type between brackets or parentheses. The **dialogue** consists of the words that the characters speak. Remembering the stage directions, try to hear the words of the dialogue as the characters might actually speak them. Notice when the punctuation calls for a pause or a change in the volume or tone of a character's voice.

Use the stage directions and dialogue to form a mental picture of the **characters**, or people in the play. If this were a live production, how would the stage look? Once you can picture the characters and the setting, try to visualize the **action** as it takes place.

After you understand the scene, try to think beyond it. What does the playwright have to say apart from the literal content? What additional **idea**, or message, does the scene convey?

The Interview

[*The scene opens in the reception room of the Wurtz Manufacturing Company. Noisily chewing a wad of bubble gum, Henry Johnson walks aimlessly around. Sometimes he sits down for a few seconds before jumping up again. He wears a gray sweater over a white shirt with a ragged collar. A big round button pinned to his sweater says "I Like Girls" in red letters.*]

HENRY: [*Nervously, in a low voice*] Do I have to wait much longer?

SECRETARY: No, Mr. Harvey should be finished in a minute.

HENRY: I'm a little nervous about interviews, you know.

5 SECRETARY: [*In a sympathetic tone*] Everyone is, so don't feel bad. Better take that gum out of your mouth, though. Mr. Harvey hates the sound of gum popping. [*Henry quickly removes his gum and drops it, unwrapped, in the secretary's ashtray. She*
10 *frowns. Meanwhile, Mr. Harvey comes out of his office. He steps up to greet Henry. They shake hands; Henry has a light grasp.*]

MR. HARVEY: [*In a firm, commanding voice*] Hello, Henry. I'm William Harvey.

15 HENRY: [*Softly*] Hello, William. Nice to meet you.

	MR. HARVEY:	[*Taken aback*] Step into my office, Henry, and we'll talk. [HENRY *sits down across from Mr. Harvey's desk.* MR. HARVEY *looks over Henry's application and then sits down.*] Well, Henry, I see you have
20		applied for the machinist's position. Tell me about your qualifications.
	HENRY:	[*Slightly confused*] Well, I can do anything. I've been a factory worker, a stock boy, an usher, a zookeeper's helper . . .
25	MR. HARVEY:	Let's stick to the position you've applied for, Henry. Do you have any experience as a machinist?
	HENRY:	Not really.
	MR. HARVEY:	Well, what about a training program?
	HENRY:	[*Brightening*] I did go to trade school.
30	MR. HARVEY:	Well, then.
	HENRY:	Uh-huh. For one solid week. [HENRY *looks serious. He closes his lips tightly.*]
	MR. HARVEY:	Is something wrong?
35	HENRY:	No, I'm just trying to keep my teeth from showing. It's a habit I have in interviews.
	MR. HARVEY:	[*Hurriedly*] Oh—Well, we'll keep your applicaton on file and call you if we need you. Thank you for coming.
40	HENRY:	You can call me at my sister's place. That's where I usually hang out, just waiting for the phone to ring. [HENRY *exits.*]

This simple scene illustrates the basic elements of drama. It is presented in the form of dialogue framed by stage directions. Characters meet and interact. There is an underlying idea that goes beyond the scene itself.

All of the conversation in this scene happens to be between characters. But there is also a type of dramatic scene in which a single character gives a speech alone upon the stage. Such a scene is called a **soliloquy**.

STAGE DIRECTIONS AND PUNCTUATION

Stage directions and punctuation provide clues to a character's emotions and actions. Stage directions are set off from dialogue by *italics*. When Henry discards his used chewing gum in the ashtray, the stage directions call for the secretary to frown, indicating her displeasure.

The stage directions involving Henry reveal his discomfort. He appears confused. He is serious about something that is laughable. He purses his lips nervously.

The punctuation in a play consists of the same marks used in prose. In addition, dashes and ellipsis points often appear in dialogue.

The *dash* (—) indicates a break, a change of direction, or an interruption. Notice how the dash following the "Oh" in line 36 emphasizes the importance of what Mr. Harvey says next. It signifies a definite change in his train of thought. It marks the moment when he decides to waste no more of his valuable time with Henry.

Ellipsis points (. . .) indicate that a character's voice just trails off. When Henry's voice stops after "zookeeper's helper" in line 24, the points of ellipsis tell you that he has lost his way. He knows he's talking too much, but he doesn't quite know how to stop. His voice just fades away into an awkward silence.

DIALOGUE

Dialogue refers to the spoken words of a play. Together, the dialogue and physical action form the basic structure of drama.

The dialogue between Henry and the secretary tells us about Henry's situation and some of his problems. The dialogue between Henry and Mr. Harvey reveals more of Henry's failings and much about Mr. Harvey's strengths. Henry is impolite, unqualified, ill at ease, and not very bright. Mr. Harvey is poised, direct, and decisive.

No less important than the dialogue in a play is just how the words are spoken. Try to hear the voices of the characters. What do they sound like? Henry's voice is unsure and shy. At first, the secretary's voice is sympathetic.

Stage directions often specify the characteristics of a voice. These include volume, pitch, and tone. The **volume** of a voice is how loud or soft it is. **Pitch** refers to a musical quality. Is the voice pitched high or low? What does a high-pitched voice suggest or reveal about a person? What about a deep voice? **Tone** is an emotional quality that reflects a character's mood. The tone of someone's voice determines whether a simple sentence like "This is great!" means exactly what it says or just the opposite.

CHARACTER

As you already know, a character's personality and motives are revealed by the person's words and actions, thoughts and feelings, and by the author's description of the character.

A playwright reveals dramatic character through dialogue, action, and description. In a play, everything you see and hear onstage is important. You are supposed to draw inferences from the appearance of the characters, from their voices, costumes, manner of speaking, and even from the sets. You miss out on some important elements of a play when you read it instead of seeing and hearing it performed. When you read drama, it's important to pay close attention to the stage directions and dialogue.

The stage directions in *The Interview* reveal how unattractive Henry is. He dresses tastelessly. His manners are poor. His appearance and conduct reveal him to be immature and lacking in common sense. Even Mr. Harvey, a model of poise and tact, is visibly "taken aback" when Henry addresses him by his first name. Mr. Harvey's statements and actions reveal him to be friendly, self-assured, and businesslike.

When you see a play onstage, you learn what a character's thoughts and feelings are by how that character speaks and acts. Body language, tone of voice, and visual and vocal expression reveal a character's true thoughts and feelings. The acting is crucial.

When you read a play, however, you must rely on the dialogue and stage directions. You also need to recognize scenes that have special importance. When, for example, a character speaks to a confidant (someone he trusts), he is more likely to reveal his real predicament or his true feelings. In *The Interview*, the secretary functions as Henry's confidant. Henry tells her how nervous he is, something he would not express to Mr. Harvey.

A character's ***motivation*** explains why he behaves as he does. When the secretary gives Henry reassurance and good advice, she is motivated by sympathy. She understands how uncomfortable a job interview can be. But, like many dramatic characters, she never explains her motives; you have to infer them.

A character's ***response*** is his reaction to a situation, event, or remark. How did Mr. Harvey respond when Henry addressed him rudely? Responses are often less immediate than Mr. Harvey's shock. They can develop gradually and culminate, or end, in a crucial scene.

EXERCISE 1

Directions: Read the following excerpt from a play. Then put a check in front of the correct answer to the questions that follow.

RICHARD: [*Rising*] Bunt? Two runs behind, the bases loaded and they send Hodges up to bunt! [*Shaking his head, he goes into the kitchen. He reappears carrying a bottle of raspberry soda. Still appalled.*] Bunt, for God's sake! Well, what are you going to do? [*He looks around aimlessly for a moment.*] I'm hungry. Well,
5   that's what comes of having dinner at Schrafft's! Schrafft's! I wanted to have dinner in the saloon across the street—but you can't have dinner in a saloon and then not . . . They don't like it. Oh, I suppose I could have ordered a drink and then not drunk it. . . . But I figure it's easier just to eat at Schrafft's. [*He drops wearily onto the chaise {chair}.*] It's hard on a man when the family
10   goes away. It's peaceful, though, with everybody gone. It's sure as hell peaceful. [*He settles back in the chaise and grins. Music sneaks in very softly, and the light on him dims to a spot.*] Ricky was really upset this morning when they left for the station. It was very flattering. I thought the kid was going to cry. . . . [*He sits, smiling, remembering the scene. Dream
15   lighting by the front door picks up* HELEN *and* RICKY *leaving.*]

RICKY: But what about Daddy? Isn't Daddy coming with us?

HELEN: Daddy'll come up Friday night.

RICKY: But, Mommy, why can't Daddy come up with us now?

HELEN: Poor Daddy has to stay in the hot city and make money. We're going to
20   spend the whole summer at the beach, but poor Daddy can only come up weekends.

RICKY: Poor Daddy . . .

HELEN: Daddy is going to work very hard. He's going to eat properly and not smoke like Dr. Murphy told him, and he's going to stay on the wagon for a while like
25   Dr. Summers told him, to take care of his nervous indigestion. . . .

[*In the spot,* RICHARD *drinks from the bottle of raspberry soda. He is somewhat awed by the taste. He looks curiously at the label and then reads it.*]

RICHARD: "Contains carbonated water, citric acid, corn syrup, artificial raspberry
30   flavoring, pure vegetable colors, and preservative." Since I've been on the wagon, I've had one continuous upset stomach. [*He looks sadly at the bottle and drinks some more.*]

HELEN: And just to make sure Daddy's all right, Mommy is going to call Daddy at ten o'clock tonight. . . .

35   RICKY: Poor Daddy . . .

[*The music fades and so does the dream light by the door.* HELEN *and* RICKY *disappear. The lighting returns to normal.*]

RICHARD: [*Coming out of his reverie {dream}*] Ten o'clock! I don't even know how I'm going to stay awake till ten o'clock! [*He stares moodily off into the growing dusk. Suddenly he notices something in an apartment across the court. He is momentarily fascinated and rises for a better look.*] Hey, lady! I know it's a hot night but . . . You sit out on this terrace, it's like having a television set with about thirty channels all going at once. . . . Don't give me any dirty look, lady. I pay rent for this terrace. If you don't like it, pull your blind down! [*As she apparently does so.*] Oh. Well, that's life.

—Excerpted from *The Seven Year Itch*, by George Axelrod

1. As the scene opens, what is Richard doing?

_____ **(1)** listening to a baseball game

_____ **(2)** having dinner

_____ **(3)** recalling a scene from earlier in the day

2. The phrase "stay on the wagon" (line 24) refers to

_____ **(1)** driving to work

_____ **(2)** avoiding alcohol

_____ **(3)** working late

3. The conversation between Ricky and Helen occurs

_____ **(1)** over the telephone

_____ **(2)** in another location

_____ **(3)** in Richard's memory

4. What does Richard think about Dr. Summers' advice?

_____ **(1)** He wishes he had taken it sooner.

_____ **(2)** He can hardly wait to tell Helen about it.

_____ **(3)** He thinks it has made him sick.

5. Richard has to stay awake until ten o'clock because

_____ **(1)** he wants to hear the end of the ball game

_____ **(2)** that's when Ricky and Helen will be home

_____ **(3)** he expects a phone call from Helen

ANSWERS ARE ON PAGE 208.

ACTION

The **action** of a play is comparable to the plot of a novel. As the characters interact, the story begins to unfold and dramatic conflict develops. The action builds upward, with tension increasing, to a high point, or **climax**, from which the story turns downward again, toward a conclusion.

The opening scene of *The Interview* presents Henry and the secretary in the first of a series of related events, culminating in the interview itself, which you know is destined to go badly because Henry is hopelessly unprepared.

As you follow the developments of a play, look for clues about what the **outcome**, or result, will be. Henry's admission of minimal job training practically guarantees that Mr. Harvey will reject him. Usually, however, indications of the outcome are not so obvious.

IDEA

Just as nonfiction has a main idea, and fiction has a theme, drama has an underlying message that the playwright wants to communicate to the audience. This is the **idea** of a play.

As you already know, main ideas and themes in prose are rarely, if ever, spelled out. You must infer them from the details. Likewise, in dramatic works, there is no direct statement of the underlying idea. You must infer it from the dialogue, stage directions, characterization, and action.

The dramatic elements of *The Interview* point to the idea without stating it directly. The stage directions fill out the characters of both Henry and Mr. Harvey. The purpose of the scene is told in the dialogue. The characters' interaction moves events along toward the outcome. The idea of the scene is that lacking social skills and experience, Henry has no hope of being offered a job.

Remember, though, that the idea of a play can be as complex as the play itself. *The Interview* is straightforward and uncomplicated and it is not too difficult to draw inferences from it. Most drama, however, requires that you give serious thought to understanding a play's content and meaning.

EXERCISE 2

Directions: Read the following passage from a play. Then put a check in front of the correct answer to the questions that follow.

> [*In the back room of Dave's Dive,* DAVID, CINDY, *and* MOLLY *argue.*]

	DAVID:	You skipped out on me again Friday night.
	CINDY:	[*In a pleading voice*] You know that's my prayer-meeting night.
	DAVID:	Beer and whiskey buy the bread in this house, you know.
	CINDY:	But we agreed—Friday would be my day off.
5	DAVID:	Friday is our busiest night, and your pretty little face gets a lot of guys to buy a lot of drinks. I need you here on Friday nights.
	CINDY:	[*Turning to her mother*] Tell David what it says in the Bible. Man does not live by bread alone. You know what Daddy used to say.
10	MOLLY:	Honey, Daddy is gone, and we've got to make a living now. You ate hand-to-mouth as a preacher's daughter.
	CINDY:	Maybe so—we were poor, but we were happy. Mama, why did you have to marry him anyway . . .
	MOLLY:	Stop it, Cindy. David saved us from losing everything.
15	DAVID:	[*Smiling at Cindy*] You'll be just as happy drinkin' and havin' fun with the customers.
	CINDY:	[*Crying*] I hate this place, the booze, the smoke, everything. Mama, these people are lost souls and he [*Pointing to* DAVID], he's the devil.

1. David is Cindy's

_____ **(1)** ex-husband

_____ **(2)** stepfather

_____ **(3)** husband

2. You can infer that Molly

_____ **(1)** does not care about her daughter's feelings

_____ **(2)** thinks Cindy is unreasonable

_____ **(3)** sympathizes with her daughter

3. David's attitude toward Cindy is

_____ **(1)** violent

_____ **(2)** manipulative

_____ **(3)** fatherly

4. Cindy is upset with David because he

_____ **(1)** broke an agreement

_____ **(2)** mocked her pretty face

_____ **(3)** forced her to work overtime

ANSWERS ARE ON PAGE 209.

WRITING ACTIVITY 7

Choose a character from one of the play excerpts you read in this chapter. Write a description of the character that includes his or her name, approximate age, physical features, and personality traits. Try to make the person's thoughts and feelings come alive through your description.

ANSWERS WILL VARY.

PRE-GED Practice
EXERCISE 3

Questions 1–4 refer to the following excerpt from a play.

MEL: I'm not through with my life yet . . . I still have value, I still have worth.

EDNA: What kind of a life is this? You
5 live like some kind of a caged animal in a Second Avenue zoo that's too hot in one room, too cold in another, over- charged for a growth on
10 the side of the building they call a terrace that can't support a cactus plant, let alone two human beings. Is this what you call a worthwhile
15 life? Banging on walls and jiggling toilets?

MEL: [*Shouts*] You think it's any better in sunny Spain? Go swimming on the beach, it'll
20 take you the rest of the summer to scrape the oil off.

EDNA: Forget Spain. There are other places to live.

MEL: Maine? Vermont maybe? You
25 think it's all rolling hills and maple syrup? They have more people on welfare up there than they have pancakes. Washington? Oregon?
30 Unemployed lumberjacks are sitting around sawing legs off chairs; they have nothing else to do.

EDNA: I will go anywhere in the world
35 you want to go, Mel. I will live in a cave, a hut, or a tree. I will live on a raft in the Amazon jungle if that's what you want to do.

MEL: All right, call a travel agency.
40 Get two economy seats to Bolivia. We'll go to Aber- crombie's tomorrow, get a couple of pith helmets and a
45 spear gun.

EDNA: Don't talk to me like I'm insane.

MEL: I'm halfway there, you might as well catch up.

50 EDNA: I am trying to offer reasonable suggestions. I am not responsible. I am not the one who's doing this to you.

MEL: I didn't say you were, Edna.

55 EDNA: Then what do you want from me? What do you want from anyone?

MEL: [*Buries his face in his hands*] Just a little breathing space . . . just for a little while.

60

—Excerpted from *The Prisoner of Second Avenue*, by Neil Simon

1. The main idea of this passage is Mel's

(1) asthma
(2) desire to travel
(3) unhappy marriage
(4) mental anguish
(5) aches and pains

2. Which one of the following statements about Mel is true?

(1) He is indifferent about his living situation.
(2) He feels trapped.
(3) He is dying to travel.
(4) He wants to move to another country.
(5) He is reckless.

3. Edna reacts to Mel's ramblings with

(1) frustration
(2) encouragement
(3) love
(4) indifference
(5) humor

4. Why is this play called *The Prisoner of Second Avenue*?

(1) Mel is desperate for a little escape.
(2) Mel is a prisoner in a New York jail.
(3) Edna wants a divorce.
(4) New Yorkers live behind double-locked doors.
(5) Living in Mel and Edna's building is like living in a zoo.

Questions 5–10 refer to the following excerpt from a play.

ASTON: Sleep well?

DAVIES: Yes. Dead out. Must have been dead out.

5 ASTON: [*Goes downstage right, collects the toaster and examines it.*] You . . . er . . .

DAVIES: Eh?

ASTON: Were you dreaming or something?

10 DAVIES: Dreaming?

ASTON: Yes.

DAVIES: I don't dream. I've never dreamed.

ASTON: No, nor have I.

15 DAVIES: Nor me. [*Pause*] Why you ask me that, then?

ASTON: You were making noises.

DAVIES: Who was?

ASTON: You were.

20 DAVIES: [*Gets out of bed. He wears long underpants.*] Now, wait a minute. Wait a minute, what do you mean? What kind of noises?

25 ASTON: You were making groans. You were jabbering.

DAVIES: Jabbering? Me?

ASTON: Yes.

DAVIES: I don't jabber, man. Nobody
30 ever told me that before. [*Pause*] Nobody ever told me that before. [*Pause*] You got hold of the wrong bloke, mate.

35 ASTON: [*Crossing to the bed with the toaster*] No. You woke me up. I thought you might have been dreaming.

DAVIES: I wasn't dreaming. I never
40 had a dream in my life. [*Pause*]

ASTON: Maybe it was the bed.

DAVIES: Nothing wrong with this bed.

ASTON: Might be a bit unfamiliar.

45 DAVIES: There's nothing unfamiliar about me with beds. I slept in beds. I don't make noises just because I sleep in a bed. I slept in plenty of beds.

—Excerpted from *The Caretaker,* by Harold Pinter

5. According to Aston, Davies' dreaming was

   (1) pleasant
   (2) funny
   (3) sad
   (4) interesting
   (5) disturbing

6. In line 26, the word *jabbering* means

   (1) punching
   (2) listening
   (3) screaming
   (4) babbling
   (5) dreaming

7. Davies' reaction to Aston's remarks can best be characterized as

   (1) defensive
   (2) quiet
   (3) predictable
   (4) perceptive
   (5) indifferent

8. The conversation probably takes place

   (1) in the morning
   (2) during the night
   (3) in a small town
   (4) in a large city
   (5) in the parlor

9. The British term *bloke* (line 33) means

   (1) fellow
   (2) idea
   (3) bed
   (4) dream
   (5) clothing

10. The phrase "dead out" (line 2) means

    (1) murdered
    (2) sleeping soundly
    (3) correct
    (4) quiet
    (5) dark

ANSWERS ARE ON PAGE 209.

8  Commentaries on the Arts

Most **commentaries** on the arts take the form of reviews and essays about popular culture. You are probably already familiar with reviews of movies and television. If you have ever read reviews of fiction, nonfiction, poetry, or drama, then you are also acquainted with commentaries on literature. The performing arts—music, dance, and theater—are often covered in magazines and big-city newspapers. So are the visual arts of painting, architecture, sculpture, and photography.

REVIEWS AND ESSAYS

Newspapers and magazines regularly feature **reviews** of movies, books, television, and radio. Reviews are *subjective* because the reviewers give their opinions and defend them. A review can help you decide whether you would enjoy a particular book, program, or film.

While reviews are specific to a single work, **essays** are about categories. If the subject of a movie review is *My Fair Lady,* a related essay might be about one aspect of movie musicals in general.

An **informative essay** is written for readers with no special background. On the subject of movie musicals, an informative essay might examine their history or focus on a noteworthy director or performer. The essay might analyze the process by which a book or a story is adapted for the screen. Informative essays are written to teach. They inform without judging.

A **critical essay** is written for readers who are familiar with a subject. Because they are aimed at readers who already have the basics, critical essays tend to be at a more advanced level.

A critical essay about movie musicals might focus on technique, style, or structure. It might discuss the finer points of costume, lighting, or set design. Like reviews, critical essays are subjective because the writers give their own interpretation, analysis, and personal opinions.

HOW TO READ COMMENTARIES

The best way to read reviews and essays is to keep in mind the reading skills you have already learned. Start by scanning. This will help you find the main idea. Keep the main idea in mind as you read.

If the commentary is a review or a critical essay, remember that it is an *opinion piece*. Look for the opinions. How does the author back them up?

Does the commentary include a plot summary, a description of artwork, or biographical information about an artist? If so, study such material carefully.

Think about the commentary's writing style and structure. Notice the author's choice of words and the order in which details are presented.

Form your own opinion. What do you think about the work being discussed? Is it something you would like to experience for yourself? Why? How did the main idea and supporting details influence your opinion?

The commentaries you are about to read cover a great many art forms. They will call into play all of the reading skills you have learned so far. Since reviewers and critics rely so heavily on fact, opinion, and descriptive language, this chapter also provides additional work on these elements.

FACT AND OPINION

Marian Anderson (1902–1993), one of the foremost singers of this century, was born to a poor African-American family in Philadelphia. By the time she was six years old, she was singing in the choir of the Union Baptist Church. Recognizing her exceptional voice and her family's poverty, the congregation raised the money for her to take professional voice lessons. At the age of 23 she won first place in a major singing competition and the opportunity to perform with the New York Philharmonic Orchestra, an event that launched her international career.

The preceding paragraph consists of facts that can be found in newspapers, books, or encyclopedias. Anyone can look them up. **Facts** are true statements that can be checked through research.

Opinions cannot be proved by research because they consist of interpretations and personal views. Like facts, however, opinions are an essential part of commentaries on the arts.

A problem arises when you confuse opinions with facts. Consider the following:

> Marian Anderson's rich contralto voice is unsurpassed in purity and unequaled in range. You can almost hear her old church choir pushing this shining instrument beyond the natural limits of the human voice.

The preceding paragraph is an opinion. The reviewer is writing subjectively. It is a personal judgment, not a fact, that Marian Anderson's voice has no equal in purity and range. It is a personal perception, not a fact, that one can hear in Anderson's singing the influence of the gospel choir from her childhood. It is also a personal opinion that Anderson's voice is equally strong at the extremes of its range. Other listeners, or critics, might disagree.

What *is* a fact is that the reviewer loves Anderson's voice and so has written a rave review.

As you read the commentaries in this chapter, make sure you know when you are reading facts and when you are reading opinions. Remember, a fact is something that can be researched and verified. An opinion consists of personal views, which the public and other critics may not share.

Have you ever really enjoyed a performance that the critics didn't like? Were you ever disappointed by a book that everyone else seemed to enjoy? Have you ever gone to see an award-winning film only to wonder afterward how it could have won anything? Such experiences are easy to explain. Opinions, unlike facts, differ enormously from one person to the next.

All of the statements below refer to the long-running television soap opera *All My Children*. Some of the statements are facts. Others express opinion. Even if you have never seen the show, you should have no difficulty recognizing which is which.

Write *F* for each statement that is a fact or *O* for each statement that expresses an opinion.

_____ **1.** *All My Children* is set in the fictional town of Pine Valley.

_____ **2.** With so many characters added in recent years, it has become impossible to keep track of the plot's bizarre twists and turns.

_____ **3.** The characters of Erica Kane, Dr. Joe Martin, and Ruth Martin have been part of the show since it premiered as a half-hour drama on January 5, 1970.

_____ **4.** The show was created by Agnes Nixon.

_____ **5.** Erica has more romantic chemistry with Jack than with Dimitri.

_____ **6.** Nobody could possibly replace Michael E. Knight in the role of Tad Martin.

_____ **7.** For his portrayal of twin brothers Adam and Stuart Chandler, David Canary has won the Daytime Emmy award for best actor.

_____ **8.** It must be frustrating to play a character as simple and naive as Dixie.

_____ **9.** Dixie should never have had her hair cut.

_____ **10.** Brooke English is the mother of two children, one deceased.

Statements 1, 3, 4, 7, and 10 are facts. Statements 2, 5, 6, 8, and 9 are opinions. Did you identify all of them correctly? Research can verify the accuracy of the factual statements. The opinion statements should have been easy to spot. Elements such as whether a plot is bizarre or impossible to follow, romantic chemistry between actors, if a character seems naive or simple, and the best length for someone's hair are all matters of opinion.

EXERCISE 1

Part A

Directions: Read the four reviews below. Then write *F* for each statement that is a fact or *O* for each statement that expresses an opinion.

1. ***Carousel***—"A wildly acclaimed revival of the 1945 Rodgers & Hammerstein musical about a carnival barker whose romance leads to violence and finally redemption. As contemporary as anything on Broadway. Winner of five 1994 Tony awards, including Best Musical Revival, and deserving of even more."

   —Excerpted from *New York* magazine, September 5, 1994

   _____ **(1)** *Carousel* is a revival of a 1945 musical by Rodgers and Hammerstein.

   _____ **(2)** It deserved more than the five Tony awards it won.

   _____ **(3)** It won the 1994 Tony award for Best Musical Revival.

2. ***Nunsense***—An "entertaining musical comedy, now in its ninth year, of five sensible and motivated nuns who mount a talent show to raise money for what they personally and firmly consider to be a good and noble cause."

   —Excerpted from *New York* magazine, September 5, 1994

   _____ **(1)** *Nunsense* is an entertaining musical comedy.

   _____ **(2)** The main characters are five nuns who put together a talent show.

   _____ **(3)** The show has been running for nine years.

3. ***Damn Yankees***—"A revival of the 1956 Tony-award-winning musical comedy, about a baseball fan who sells his soul to the Devil so that his favorite team can win. Director Jack O'Brien has deftly updated the book, and his visual touches are as quotably witty as his additions to the dialogue."

   —Excerpted from *New York* magazine, September 5, 1994

   _____ **(1)** *Damn Yankees* is a revival of a musical comedy first presented in 1956.

   _____ **(2)** The title of the play refers to a baseball team.

   _____ **(3)** Director Jack O'Brien has added witty new elements to the dialogue and the action.

4. *Jackie Mason: Politically Incorrect*—"Oy, is he ever! A new one-man show written and performed by Mason, who jokes ruthlessly and effectively about every touchy social issue and racial minority imaginable. He might enjoy some heckling; it would give him a chance to harangue even more."

—Excerpted from *New York* magazine, September 5, 1994

_____ **(1)** *Jackie Mason: Politically Incorrect* is a new one-man show.

_____ **(2)** Mason's jokes are ruthless and effective.

_____ **(3)** The jokes target minorities and controversial issues.

Part B

Directions: Reread the preceding four commentaries. Then, for each question below, write the number of the correct commentary.

_____ **1.** Which commentary praises the work of a musical comedy director?

_____ **2.** Which commentary is about a musical that is not a comedy?

_____ **3.** Which commentary jokingly recommends that members of the audience heckle a performer?

_____ **4.** Which commentary implies some unfairness in the awards process?

DESCRIPTIVE LANGUAGE

Commentaries on the arts are full of **descriptive language**, colorful words and phrases. The following phrases are typical of the language of reviews: *fresh and funny, delightful from beginning to end, sparkling, spellbinding; you will laugh and cry.*

What do all of the examples above have in common? They're all positive. Critics use language like this to recommend what they are reviewing.

Now look at more examples of descriptive language used in reviews: *wooden performances, shrill and preachy, needlessly crude and violent, never quite gets going, a tired rehash.*

Such is the language of bad reviews. These judgments are negative. The critics do not recommend what they have reviewed. Their language reveals some of the reasons for their disapproval.

EXERCISE 2

Directions: Read the following review. Then list five words or phrases that convey the reviewer's negative opinion of the show in the space provided.

"Comedy strikes out! This simpy sitcom about life on a major-league baseball team was launched just weeks after the actual baseball fraternity went on strike. But this show has worse problems than bad timing. Take, for instance, bad writing, cardboard characters and witless plots."

—Excerpted from *People* magazine, October 10, 1994

1. _____

2. _____

3. _____

4. _____

5. _____

ANSWERS ARE ON PAGE 209.

EXERCISE 3

Directions: Read the following reviews about the Chicago production of the play *Angels in America*. Then, in the space provided, find and write the positive adjectives and adverbs that praise the play.

"A remarkable, richly imagined odyssey"

—Richard Christiansen, *Chicago Tribune*

"Daring, bold, ruthlessly comical and intellectually stimulating"

—Roy Leonard, WGN Radio/TV

"The finest ensemble performance on any Chicago stage in years"

—Sherman Kaplan, WBBM Radio

"Every bit as effective as the Broadway production"

—Tom Valeo, *Daily Herald*

1. _____
2. _____
3. _____
4. _____
5. _____
6. _____
7. _____
8. _____

ANSWERS ARE ON PAGE 209.

EXERCISE 4

Directions: Read the following five short excerpts from reviews of the movie *The River Wild*. Then answer the questions that follow in the space provided.

The River Wild is a thrilling movie. A personal triumph for Meryl Streep. I wouldn't be surprised if she is nominated for a raft of honors."

—Gene Shalit, NBC-TV, *Today* show

"A superior thriller in every way, with brilliant performances by Meryl Streep and Kevin Bacon"

—Michael Medved, *Sneak Previews*

"A smart, spunky Meryl Streep triumphs."

—*Time* magazine

"A heart-pounding adventure, if ever there was one! Meryl Streep reveals a new dimension of her acting dynamic. An excellent performance."

—David Sheehan, KCBS-TV

"Tense, satisfying entertainment. The fun and the power come from Meryl Streep's newly robust heart . . . a fiercely convincing matriarchal action hero."

—David Ansen, *Newsweek* magazine

1. What two words does the *Time* review use to describe Streep?

_____

2. What two words does David Sheehan use to describe the type of adventure found in the film?

_____

3. Which play on words does Gene Shalit use to say what he thinks Streep deserves for her performance in the film?

_____

4. Which two positive phrases does Michael Medved use to describe the film and Streep's and Bacon's acting in the film?

_____

ANSWERS ARE ON PAGE 209.

EXERCISE 5

Directions: Read the following excerpts from reviews of *The Iowa Baseball Confederacy*, a novel by W. P. Kinsella. Then match the name of the newspaper on the left with the correct descriptions on the right. Write the letters on the line provided.

"Baseball fantasy, but fantasy with substance, the power of dreams . . . One of the best books of the year."

—*Milwaukee Journal*

"A riveting mystery with a host of fascinating characters, a first-rate ghost story"

—*Detroit Free Press*

"With dazzling imagery, Kinsella explores the subtleties of the game . . . and turn-of-the-century small town America."

—*Sport* magazine

_____ **1.** *Milwaukee Journal*

_____ **2.** *Detroit Free Press*

_____ **3.** *Sport* magazine

(a) riveting mystery

(b) dazzling imagery

(c) fascinating characters

(d) fantasy with substance

(e) one of the best books of the year

(f) the power of dreams

(g) first-rate ghost story

(h) explores the subtleties of the game

ANSWERS ARE ON PAGE 210.

RADIO AND TELEVISION

In the next section, you will read commentaries about radio and television. The first article is by Jack Benny, whose radio career began in 1932 and who brought his radio program to television in 1950. He talks about the transition from radio to television.

The second excerpt is from an article by Larry Gelbart, who was the creator and writer of the award-winning television show *M*A*S*H*. In the article, he describes how the show changed during the 1974–75 season, and its third year on the air.

≡ PRE-GED Practice ≡
EXERCISE 6

Questions 1–7 are based on the passage below.

I learned, first of all, that if you're going to do a television show you should keep it to yourself. The minute your plans are known, all your friends
5 generously dedicate themselves to giving you the benefit of their experience.

I made the mistake of announcing my entrance into television several
10 weeks ahead of time. They were all ready for me. When I arrived in New York to start rehearsals, who should be at Grand Central [train station] to meet me but Eddie Cantor. Being my friend
15 and having already absorbed the vast experience of two appearances before video cameras, he felt it was his moral obligation to be the first to explain to me the facts of life in television. All the
20 way through the station, he kept jumping up and down, telling me what to do and what to avoid.

When we got into the cab, Milton Berle [a well-known comedian] was
25 sitting there waiting for us. He said he'd left his rehearsal just to come down and give me some technical advice. And then, in a few thousand well-chosen words, he briefed me on the art of how
30 to close your eyes when getting hit with a pie.

Unfortunately, as Miltie was tapering off, the cab had to stop for a red light on Forty-fifth Street. It was just
35 long enough for Jimmy Durante [another well-known comedian] to jump in with the warning that, "When youse is in television, youse is gotta speak distinkly."

40 By this time the taxi was so crowded I could hardly hear the meter. Fortunately, the three of them were so busy expounding their theories that I was able to slip out unnoticed at Forty-
45 ninth and Broadway.

But that was only the beginning of a siege of helpful advice that didn't let up until the curtain rose on my show. The only ones who didn't have
50 suggestions for my first television program were my writers.

Another thing I discovered about television is that there are far too many distractions for the studio audience. On

55 radio comedy shows, we learned a long time ago that the laughter of the studio audience has a direct effect on the home listeners' appreciation of the program. Consequently, everything

60 humanly possible is done to direct the attention of those in the audience to the person who is delivering the lines.

On a TV comedy program, the reaction of the studio audience is

65 equally important to its success. But with television, there is not only the frequent distraction of stagehands moving and sometimes dropping props as they get ready for the next scene,

70 but the sets are so constructed that those in the studio inevitably miss half of what is going on. What little they might otherwise see is often obscured by the three cameramen, usually hefty,

75 whose bulk hovers between the studio audience and the performers on stage. Fortunately I had been warned about this condition, and when the time came for me to select a cameraman for my

80 show, my first question was not "How good is he?" but "How much does he weigh?"

The things I have just mentioned are a few of the discouraging aspects

85 of the present television scene. But, on the whole, I was amazed at the phenomenal progress that this infant industry has already made.

I found that the technicians not

90 only have a high degree of competence, but that they face the problems that are constantly cropping up with speed, skill, and imagination. Some of the sets that I saw constructed in a few hours would

95 do credit to a $3 million movie pro-

duction. The directors, despite a lack of time, space, and facilities, are staging scenes day after day that it would take Hollywood weeks to duplicate.

100 And the cameramen do more than get in the way of the studio audience. On a live television show, there is no such thing as a retake. It has to be right the first time. And yet, with a very few

105 hours of rehearsal for their benefit, these cameramen somehow manage to shoot even hour-long dramatic shows without noticeable mistakes. If it is true that TV has borrowed from the

110 techniques of movie making, it is also true that the movie industry would do well, even at this early stage, to adapt many of the streamlined methods of television.

—Excerpted from *Jack Benny: The Radio and Television Work,* by the Museum of Television and Radio

1. When Jack Benny said, "If you're going to do a television show you should keep it to yourself," he was referring to a

   (1) fear of performing on television
   (2) need to come up with his own ideas
   (3) lot of unnecessary advice he got from friends
   (4) preference for working on radio instead of television
   (5) mistrust of writers' ideas

2. Benny's opinion of television technicians is that they

   (1) interfered with the home audience's enjoyment of a show
   (2) would benefit from exercise since they were overweight
   (3) showed great creativity in dealing with problems as they arose
   (4) designed sets better suited to movies
   (5) did not know about moviemaking techniques

3. Benny expresses the opinion that the movie industry

   (1) spends too much money on producing sets
   (2) should be more careful in its selection of cameramen
   (3) lacks creative directors
   (4) needs more imaginative writers
   (5) could learn a lot from the television industry

4. The tone of Benny's article can best be described as

   (1) insincere and joking
   (2) humorous and informative
   (3) distant and serious
   (4) forced and rehearsed
   (5) discouraged and regretful

5. The term *duplicate* (line 99) means

   (1) trick
   (2) copy
   (3) send
   (4) admire
   (5) imagine

6. The term *phenomenal* (line 87) means

   (1) fortunate
   (2) laughable
   (3) slow
   (4) remarkable
   (5) problematic

7. "And then, in a few thousand well-chosen words, he [Milton Berle] briefed me on the art of how to close your eyes when getting hit with a pie" is an example of

   (1) literal language
   (2) figurative language
   (3) comedic expression
   (4) technical advice
   (5) rehearsal directions

ANSWERS ARE ON PAGE 210.

EXERCISE 7

Directions: Read the passage below and then answer the questions that follow.

Between Years Two and Three—that would have been in 1974—Gene [producer Gene Reynolds] and I went to Korea, and I think the show very much reflected that trip. If, indeed, the stories got better in Year Three, it's because of this trip. We went to the 8055 [the mobile army surgical hospital on which *M*A*S*H* was based and] which, of course,
5 was no longer mobile and, as you know, was the real hospital where Dr. Richard Hornberger was stationed. We talked to everybody and came back with twenty-two hours of taped conversations—nurses, doctors, chopper pilots. We even found an orderly who had been there during the war and who remembered some of the doctors. We got a taste of the real thing, and it was very hard to come back and be funny after that. It was also
10 hard to separate fact from what we were doing on screen, and it's that marriage that I think is what really made the difference in Years Three and Four. It was an enormous recharge for us to go, to be able to do this research, to come back with these notes. When you actually go to Korea and see a soldier without hands and feet lying in bed, you have something to mull over [think about] for a long, long while.

15 The strength of the Third Year was also a reflection of our strength with the network. We were finally secure; we had ratings; we had less trouble with the censors; we were able to do much more of what we wanted to do. We'd had two years of experience with the characters, the format; we knew what was working, what audiences would take in terms of heavy material mixed with their comedy. Suddenly we were winners, an overnight
20 success story with an overnight that happened to have lasted two years.

—Excerpted from *The Complete Book of M*A*S*H,* by Suzy Kalter

1. Larry Gelbart says that if "the stories got better in Year Three, [it was] because of this trip." Where did he travel?

_____

2. What was the 8055?

_____

3. How did the 8055 change between the Korean War and the time of Gelbart's visit?

_____

4. During his trip, Gelbart taped more than 20 hours of conversations with

_____

5. After seeing "the real thing," Gelbart found it more difficult to

_____

6. You can infer that during its first two years on television, *M*A*S*H*

_____

7. What do the letters *M.A.S.H.* stand for?

_____

8. What role did Reynolds play in the creation of *M*A*S*H*?

_____

9. Name four reasons the third year of the television show became much stronger.

_____

_____

ANSWERS ARE ON PAGE 210.

THE PERFORMING ARTS

In the next section, you will read about a distinguished American actor and a legendary Broadway musical. The first passage is about Paul Robeson, who first came to public attention in 1924, when he starred in two plays written by Eugene O'Neill: *The Emperor Jones* and *All God's Chillun Got Wings*.

The second commentary is about a new 1994 production of the 1927 musical *Show Boat*, created by composer Jerome Kern and lyricist Oscar Hammerstein II.

EXERCISE 8

Directions: Read the passage below about the career of Paul Robeson, one of the finest actors of his day. Then answer the questions that follow.

[His starring role in the play *All God's Chillun Got Wings*] made Robeson famous. Critics exclaimed over his movements, his expressive features, his resonant voice. He was soon giving concerts of spirituals and black work songs at the Provincetown Playhouse, and he quickly became nearly as famous for his singing as he was for his acting. In fact,
5 O'Neill [playwright Eugene O'Neill] and the Provincetown director, James Light, added a black spiritual to one of the jungle scenes in *The Emperor Jones*. When that play began its second run, Robeson's importance as an actor was increased. In 1925, he went to London with the production, thus becoming the first black American dramatic actor to play on the English stage since Ira Aldridge had played Othello there over a half century
10 earlier.

But here the comparison between Robeson and Aldridge ended. Robeson hadn't had enough stage experience to be considered a trained actor, as he was the first to admit. His real skill was singing, a discipline he preferred. When white critics pronounced him a "natural actor," neither he nor blacks who knew anything about acting were pleased. It was
15 like saying that blacks had natural rhythm or were natural athletes. Whites seemed unable to admit that blacks could work and train hard to be good at what they did.

Paul Robeson's next role was that of a black prizefighter in *Black Boy*, a play by two white writers. He then toured in the musical play *Show Boat*. Although neither play did much for his acting reputation, the stage experience he gained made him better prepared
20 to play Othello in London. The play opened in 1930. Robeson now had six years of stage experience. He was also older. He brought a tremendous sensitivity to the role, and London critics raved about his "dignity, simplicity and true passion." Although Robeson would forever after be identified with the character of Brutus Jones even more so than Gilpin because Robeson also appeared in the film version of the play, his favorite role and
25 the one he felt he played best was that of Othello.

The next time Robeson performed as Shakespeare's tragic hero was thirteen years later. He was now forty-five years old and very experienced. He'd appeared in several motion pictures, a few more plays, and had spent nearly ten years giving concerts all over Europe. Mature and dignified, he brought these qualities to that demanding role in an
30 unforgettable way. His portrayal of Othello in the American Theatre Guild production of the play was not only a high point in his career but also a high point in the history of the American theater. *Othello* opened at the Shubert Theater on October 19, 1943, and ran until July 1, 1944, playing to packed houses for 296 consecutive performances, a record run for Shakespeare in New York.

—Excerpted from *Black Theater in America*, by James Haskins

Put a check in front of the correct answer to questions 1–3.

1. The subject of this passage is

_____ **(1)** Paul Robeson's development as an actor

_____ **(2)** Paul Robeson's singing career

_____ **(3)** the history of black theater

2. It can be inferred that Brutus Jones is

_____ **(1)** a historical figure

_____ **(2)** the title character in Eugene O'Neill's *The Emperor Jones*

_____ **(3)** a character in *Othello*

3. The high point of Paul Robeson's dramatic career was

_____ **(1)** starring in *All God's Chillun Got Wings*

_____ **(2)** playing Othello in the American Theatre Guild production

_____ **(3)** being called "a natural actor"

4. Put the following events in order by numbering them from 1 to 5.

_____ Paul Robeson starred as Othello in London.

_____ Robeson became the first black American actor to appear on the English stage in half a century.

_____ The American Theatre Guild production of *Othello* opened in New York.

_____ Robeson toured in *Show Boat*.

_____ Robeson began peforming concerts of spirituals and work songs.

5. List five words or phrases used to describe the acting genius of Paul Robeson.

_____

_____

_____

ANSWERS ARE ON PAGE 210.

EXERCISE 9

Directions: Read the passage below and answer the questions that follow.

It's easy to say what's wrong with *Show Boat,* the 1927 musical by composer Jerome Kern and lyricist Oscar Hammerstein II. Based on Edna Ferber's novel about a floating theater on the Mississippi River, the show has always been too long. The most winning characters, the light-skinned black Julie and her white husband Steve, disappear
5   before the intermission. The second act, overloaded with coincidences, rambles on, covering a period from 1889 to 1927. Over the years, some critics have found the treatment of blacks patronizing and often racist. And in a dozen stage and film versions, the show has been hacked, squeezed, and revised nearly out of existence.

This week Harold Prince's new production of *Show Boat* steamed onto Broadway in
10 an $8.5 million blaze of spectacular stagecraft. And theatergoers who see this wonderfully imaginative new production can ignore all the criticism above. Handsomely cast for both musical and dramatic effect, lavishly constructed by set designer Eugene Lee and brightly conducted by Jeffrey Huard, this *Show Boat* is a near perfect staging of the work that half a century ago signaled the maturity of American musical theater. The alleged racial bias
15 in the plot, which brought some protests during the tryout of the Toronto production last year, is nowhere to be found here. To see *Show Boat* is to experience how powerful the Broadway ideal can be in the hands of a master like Prince.

—Adapted from *Time* magazine, October 10, 1994

Part A

Match each person on the left with his or her contribution on the right. Write the correct letter on the line.

_____ **1.** Eugene Lee   **(a)** produced the 1994 Broadway revival of *Show Boat*

_____ **2.** Oscar Hammerstein II   **(b)** wrote the book upon which the musical is based

_____ **3.** Edna Ferber   **(c)** conducted the orchestra for the 1994 production

_____ **4.** Harold Prince   **(d)** designed the sets for the 1994 production

_____ **5.** Jeffrey Huard   **(e)** wrote the original music for *Show Boat*

_____ **6.** Jerome Kern   **(f)** wrote the words to the songs in *Show Boat*

1. Briefly describe the setting of this play.

_____

_____

2. Over the years, the show has been criticized for all of the following EXCEPT

_____ **(1)** too many coincidences

_____ **(2)** a rambling second act

_____ **(3)** racism

_____ **(4)** its cost

3. With which of the following statements about the 1994 Broadway production of *Show Boat* would the author of this passage agree?

_____ **(1)** At $8.5 million, it cost far too much to produce.

_____ **(2)** It's not as good as the earlier Toronto production.

_____ **(3)** The sets were somewhat disappointing.

_____ **(4)** It's a masterful job by Harold Prince.

4. List four positive phrases the writer uses to review *Show Boat*.

_____

_____

_____

_____

ANSWERS ARE ON PAGE 210.

THE VISUAL ARTS

In this section, you will read commentaries about the arts of painting and photography. The first is about the work of famous impressionist painter Vincent Van Gogh. The second reviews an exhibition of Lotte Jabobi's photographs.

EXERCISE 10

Directions: Read the passage below and answer the questions that follow in the space provided.

From 1888–1889, the artist Vincent Van Gogh lived in the south of France, in the little town of Arles. Here, despite illness, he worked with great energy, producing paintings and drawings at an astonishing rate. He experimented with new ways of using color, and with different styles and subjects. This period has been described as both the height of his
5 career and a turning point in the history of Western art.

In letters from Arles to his family and friends, Van Gogh described his ideas, his health, and his work. While painting what has become a very famous picture of his bedroom, Van Gogh wrote:

"I have been and still am nearly half-dead from the past week's work. So I am forced
10 to be quiet. I have just slept sixteen hours at a stretch, and it has restored me considerably. . . ."

"Today I am all right again. My eyes are still tired, but then I had a new idea in my head and here is the sketch of it. This time it's just simply my bedroom, only here color is to do everything. The finished picture should suggest rest or sleep in general. In a word,
15 looking at the picture ought to rest the brain, or rather the imagination. The walls are pale violet. The floor is of red tiles. The wood of the bed and chairs is the yellow of fresh butter, the sheets and pillows very light greenish citron [yellow]. The bedspread scarlet. The window green. The dressing table orange, the basin blue. The doors lilac. And that is all— there is nothing in this room with its closed shutters. The broad lines of the furniture
20 again must express completed and undisturbed rest. Portraits on the walls, and a mirror and a towel and some clothes. The frame—as there is no white in the picture—will be white. I shall work on it again all day, but you see how simple the conception [idea] is. By means of all these diverse tones I have wanted to express an *absolute restfulness.*"

—Excerpted from *The Complete Letters of Vincent Van Gogh,* by Vincent Van Gogh, in *Van Gogh in Arles,* by Ronald Pickvance

1. In which town and country did Van Gogh paint the bedroom described in the passage?

_____

2. The description of the painting was written by

_____

3. Write two phrases from Van Gogh's own words that tell something about the state of his health.

_____

_____

4. What did Van Gogh want the painting of his bedroom to express?

_____

5. Van Gogh chose many bright colors to express his image. Which colors would you have used? Explain why.

_____

_____

6. With which three elements did Van Gogh experiment in his paintings during this period?

_____

7. Which color is NOT used in Van Gogh's painting of his bedroom?

_____

8. For which two reasons does Van Gogh describe himself as "nearly half-dead"?

_____

ANSWERS ARE ON PAGE 210.

EXERCISE 11

Directions: Read the selection below. Then answer the questions that follow in the space provided.

Jacobi (1896–1990) began her career in Berlin in the late twenties, as a portrait painter of poets, singers, actors, and dancers. She spent the last decades of her life in New Hampshire, continuing to photograph people she admired—Robert Frost, May Sarton, and Edward Steichen, among others. She was an enthusiastic artist who
5   recorded the spirit and creativity of the century. It is impossible to know the true extent of her achievement; she had to abandon her studio when she fled Germany in 1935, and much of her work was lost or destroyed in the war.

Lotte Jacobi has left a body of work that is memorable not only for what—and whom—it captured, but for the way the portraits reveal the essence of their subjects. "My
10 style is the style of the people I photograph," she once said. Magazines and newspapers counted on her for this openness, and her subjects came to trust her, too. When *Life* wanted to do a story on Albert Einstein, the physicist asked that she be the photographer, and no wonder. Her shots, from the twenties, of Einstein on his sailboat in Germany have an air of naturalness and intimacy; so do the portraits she took many years later in his
15 office at Princeton University. He seems completely at home. But perhaps it is Jacobi's self-portrait, taken when she was in her mid-thirties, that most clearly shows her passion for the art form that occupied her attention for over sixty years. She appears to be rushing into the picture frame, her hair flying a bit and her eyes alight.

—Adapted from *The New Yorker,* September 12, 1994

1. Where did Lotte Jacobi begin her career?

_____

2. What kinds of people did she photograph?

_____

3. What does it mean that Lotte Jacobi "recorded the spirit and creativity of the century?"

_____

4. Name four individuals whom Lotte Jacobi photographed.

_____   _____

_____   _____

5. What does the writer say Jacobi's self-portrait reveals about her?

_____

ANSWERS ARE ON PAGE 211.

LITERATURE

In the following section, you will read a commentary on poetry and one on literature. The first describes what poetry is all about. The second passage is from a review of the book *Second Chances* by Randi Jacobs.

≡ PRE-GED Practice ≡
EXERCISE 12

Directions: Read the passage below and answer the questions that follow on the next page.

What Is Poetry?

Poetry should be a deep delight, which you would enjoy as you enjoy a day in Spring, when the sun is rising, the birds are singing, and the first
5   flowers of the year are discovered along the edge of the woods. You must not think of it as a school subject about which you will be questioned one day; you must not even think of it as
10 "literature" which is an ugly word invented by schoolmasters. Poetry is like the bird's song, but since it is sung by a human being, it has more meaning, and that meaning is given in
15 words.

But the words which the poet finds—and he finds them like flowers in his path: he does not look for them— these words are special words. Some of
20 them are sweetly musical, words that are thrilling to the tongue as we utter them; others are magical words that fill the mind with wonder. Music and magic are both present in the best poems,
25 and together they give us the particular delight of poetry.

But that delight is not always simple delight—some poems make us sad, because they are about sorrow or
30 death; others make us thoughtful, because they tell us what the poet thinks about life or about the many things that happen in life. Such subjects are not forbidden, but just as a clear
35 stream will break into cloudy froth when it meets rough rocks, so thought dims the brightness of pure poetry. Poetry is not made by taking thought about a subject; rather it forms in the mind like a
40 crystal; its words are like snowflakes that fall on a green leaf. Such an event is rare, and the perfect poems in any language are so few that they could all be included in a book much smaller
45 than the Bible.

—Excerpted from *This Way, Delight*, by Herbert Read

1. What simile is used in the first paragraph?

   (1) "an ugly word invented by schoolmasters"
   (2) "poetry is like the bird's song"
   (3) "the first flowers of the year are discovered"
   (4) "poetry should be a deep delight"
   (5) "a day in Spring, when the sun is rising"

2. According to the author, what do the best poems have in common?

   (1) music and magic
   (2) birdsong and music
   (3) music and literature
   (4) thought and emotion
   (5) magic and deep thought

3. What is the main idea of this selection?

   (1) The best poetry is characterized by clear thinking.
   (2) The wrong word can spoil a poem.
   (3) Poetry needs images of nature.
   (4) Some poems are sad and thoughtful.
   (5) Reading poetry should be a joyful experience.

4. You can infer that the author advises against thinking of poetry as a school subject because

   (1) poetry is too hard to understand
   (2) poetry is so easy it doesn't need to be studied
   (3) schools already have too many other subjects to teach
   (4) the delight of poetry will be lost
   (5) children are too young to understand poetry

   ANSWERS ARE ON PAGE 211.

EXERCISE 13

Directions: Read the following review of a novel. Then answer the questions in the space provided.

When Randi Jacobs submitted her novel, *Second Chances*, the publishers should have had second thoughts. The book probably was intended to be a funny tale about the amusingly awkward romance between two middle-aged people. Instead, it is an unlikely story about two uninteresting characters.

5   A real story might have gotten in the way of the all-too-frequent jokes. Meeting in a small Ohio town, Elliot and Eloise try to get to know each other by telling endless humorous stories about themselves. Unfortunately, Jacob's characters communicate, even fight, only by using drawn-out bad puns. They talk and talk and talk, and they never laugh at each other or at their own worn-out jokes.

10   The reader never gets a chance to know what brings these two people together. In fact, it becomes all too clear why neither was married before. Apart from having pointless conversations that may generate a mild giggle, the couple never does anything. They aren't even as substantial as the floppy disks they were no doubt stored on.

15   Jacobs has managed to turn tension and humor in Smallville into a snooze in Dullsville. Elliot and Eloise had the potential to become something other than cardboard characters. Yet as is, they are paper-thin. Their problems and solutions could have entertained. Instead, their only active role might be to discourage middle-age romance.

1. What is the setting for this story?

_____

2. What is the topic of this book?

_____

3. What is the critic's opinion of *Second Chances*?

_____

4. List four phrases that indicate this critic's bias.

_____

_____

_____

_____

5. Would you accept this critic's opinion of the book as reliable? Why or why not?

_____

ANSWERS ARE ON PAGE 211.

WRITING ACTIVITY 8

    In a newspaper or magazine, find a cartoon with few words or none at all. Make sure to choose a single drawing, not a comic strip. Write a paragraph or two describing the cartoon for a friend who didn't see it. Use descriptive language to help your friend picture the cartoon as it actually looks and understand its message.

ANSWERS WILL VARY

▤ PRE-GED Practice ▤
EXERCISE 14

Questions 1–6 refer to the following excerpt from a review of an art exhibition.

The liveliness and color of Latino culture, its music, food, art and style, lend a layer of richness to Chicago culture we often take for granted in a
5 city already thick with ethnic diversity. So the excitement generated by "Images and Objects of the Spirit," the new show at the Aldo Castillo Gallery, offers a welcome opportunity to focus
10 clearly on the best of Latino art.

An eclectic [mixed] presentation of contemporary [current] Latin American fine art mixed together with furniture, textiles and religious artifacts from
15 Colombia, Guatemala, Mexico and Peru, the show offers a concentrated look into a culture steeped in religion, political conflict and passion. . . .

Aldo Castillo describes his labor of
20 love as a gallery with a social mission. An established Nicaraguan sculptor, Castillo left his homeland to escape civil war and received political asylum in the United States where he continued his
25 studies at the Art Institute of Chicago. Originally intending to create a sculpture studio, he decided instead to turn his beautiful rehabbed space in Lakeview into a gallery where he
30 could showcase his own work and that of fellow Latino artists.

The result is a glorious crash course in Latino visual arts. Contemporary work by painters

35 Antonio Bou and Luis Fernando Uribe hang over rough-hewn cabinets. Ceremonial garments woven in bright hot colors are laid about among religious objects. . . .

40 Some of the most stunning pieces in the show are the humblest. Simple retablos, small carved wooden niches designed to hold images of saints, are both rough and powerful.

—Excerpted from the *Chicago Sun-Times,* October 21, 1994

1. "Images and Objects of the Spirit" is the title of a(n)
   (1) sculpture collection
   (2) collecton of retablos
   (3) exhibition featuring Chicago artists
   (4) exhibition featuring Latino artists
   (5) one-man show

2. All of the following statements about Aldo Castillo are true EXCEPT
   (1) He is a sculptor born in Nicaragua.
   (2) His studio is devoted to ancient art.
   (3) His gallery presents the work of Latino artists.
   (4) He studied at the Art Institute of Chicago.
   (5) He considers religious objects a form of art.

3. The reviewer describes the retablos in the show as

(1) complicated
(2) political and passionate
(3) ethnically diverse
(4) rough and powerful
(5) brightly colored

4. Antonio Bou and Luis Fernando Uribe are best described as contemporary

(1) painters
(2) sculptors
(3) cabinetmakers
(4) Peruvian weavers
(5) gallery owners

5. You can infer that the reviewer

(1) enthusiastically recommends this exhibition
(2) is not familiar with Castillo's work
(3) prefers ceremonial garments to paintings and sculpture
(4) found the exhibit disappointing
(5) is reluctant to give a personal opinion

6. The exhibit presents works of art from all of the following places EXCEPT

(1) Colombia
(2) Honduras
(3) Peru
(4) Guatemala
(5) Mexico

Questions 7–11 on the next page refer to the following review of Andrew Chaikin's book *A Man on the Moon: The Voyages of the Apollo Astronauts*.

The Apollo program sent twenty-four men to the moon, among them Neil A. Armstrong, who, twenty-five years ago this month, accomplished his
5 famed "giant leap for mankind" by taking the first human step on lunar soil. Twelve of the astronauts walked on the moon—the rest flew around it—and their tasks progressed from the
10 demonstration that a lunar visit could be safely concluded to far-ranging scientific explorations of the moon's surface. Chaikin's narrative of the Apollo voyages, based on extensive interviews
15 with the astronauts, is riveting—especially his account of Apollo 13, the mission that turned into a cliff-hanger when an oxygen tank exploded, crippling the spaceship on its way to the
20 moon. He brings the astronauts to life, stripping away the gray cloak of all-American squareness in which NASA dressed them, and revealing the bright colors of their personalities and the
25 fears and exhilaration [excitement] of their remarkable journeys. They brought high competence and courage to a feat that rested on a vast political and technological enterprise. After the first
30 couple of moon walks, public interest plummeted [fell], and, once it became evident that the Soviet Union had opted out of the moon race, support for Apollo dissolved. Chaikin calls the Apollo

35 program "the last great act this country has undertaken out of a sense of optimism," whereas in truth it was one of the greatest acts America undertook—and would sustain—only in
40 response to the goad [pressure] of Cold War competition.

—Excerpted from *The New Yorker*, August 1, 1994

7. The word *riveting* (line 15) means

(1) exciting to read
(2) mechanical
(3) boring
(4) technical
(5) advanced

8. The writer obtained much information from

(1) personal experience
(2) extensive interviews with the *Apollo* astronauts
(3) NASA
(4) Cold War documents
(5) classified information

9. Which of the following expresses the reviewer's opinion?

(1) The *Apollo* program sent 24 men to the moon.
(2) Neil Armstrong took the first human step on lunar soil.
(3) The *Apollo* program was kept going only in response to the pressure of Cold War competition.
(4) The astronauts demonstrated great competence.
(5) Public interest in the *Apollo* program fell after the Soviet Union dropped out of the moon race.

10. The reviewer praises the writer for

(1) revealing the astronauts' true personalities
(2) revealing an act of American optimism
(3) criticizing NASA
(4) explaining complex experiments
(5) rekindling the public's interest in America's space program

11. The *Apollo 13* mission is described as a "cliff-hanger" because

(1) the ship landed on a rocky ledge on the moon's surface
(2) an oxygen tank exploded in flight
(3) it carried 24 astronauts
(4) the astronauts aboard had strong personalities
(5) it almost collided with a Soviet ship in deep space

Questions 12–16 refer to the following excerpt from Roger Ebert's review of the movie *Hoop Dreams*.

A film like *Hoop Dreams* is what the movies are for. It takes us, shakes us, and makes us think in new ways about the world around us. It gives us
5 the impression of having touched life itself.

Hoop Dreams is, on one level, a documentary about two African-American kids named William Gates
10 and Arthur Agee, from Chicago's inner city, who are gifted basketball players and dream of someday starring in the NBA. On another level, it is about much larger subjects: about ambition,
15 competition, race and class in our society. About our value structures. And about the daily lives of people like the Agee and Gates families, who are usually invisible in the mass media, but
20 have a determination and resiliency [staying power] that is a cause for hope.

The movie spans six years in the lives of William and Arthur, starting when they are in the eighth grade, and
25 continuing through the first year of college. It was intended originally to be a 30-minute short, but as the filmmakers followed their two subjects, they realized this was a much larger,
30 and longer story. And so we are allowed to watch the subjects grow up during the movie, and this palpable [almost physical] sense of the passage of time is like walking for a time in their shoes.

35 They're spotted during playground games by a scout for St. Joseph's High School in west suburban Westchester, a basketball powerhouse. Attending classes there will mean a long daily
40 commute to a school with few other black faces, but there's never an instant when William or Arthur, or their families, doubt the wisdom of this opportunity: St. Joseph's, we hear time and again, is
45 the school where another inner-city kid, Isiah Thomas, started his climb to NBA stardom.

—Excerpted from the *Chicago Sun-Times*, October 21, 1994

12. Which rating would the reviewer give this film (one star being the lowest rating and four stars the highest)?

  (1) one
  (2) two
  (3) two and a half
  (4) three
  (5) four

13. The reviewer says this is a film about

  (1) ambition and competition
  (2) race and class
  (3) value structures
  (4) the ordinary lives of ordinary people
  (5) all of the above

14. The main subjects of the movie are

  (1) college athletes
  (2) NBA stars
  (3) invisible families
  (4) fictional teenagers
  (5) real kids

15. You can infer that the reviewer is recommending this film for

  (1) all audiences
  (2) professional athletes only
  (3) urban audiences only
  (4) sports fans only
  (5) high school students only

16. The last paragraph implies that Arthur and William will

  (1) adjust easily to St. Joseph's
  (2) reach the NBA just as Isiah Thomas did
  (3) face problems at their new school
  (4) abandon their dreams when they are older
  (5) find many friends at St. Joseph's

ANSWERS ARE ON PAGE 211.

The Post-Test consists of 40 multiple-choice questions. It should give you a good idea of how well you have studied in this book. You should take the Post-Test only after you have completed all the chapters. Work as quickly and as carefully as you can. If a question seems too difficult, make an educated guess.

Record your answers on the answer grid on this page. Choose the best of five answer choices by filling in the corresponding circle on the answer grid.

Using the Evaluation Chart on page 199, circle the number of each question that you missed to determine which areas you might need to review before you move on to Contemporary Books' *GED Test 4: Literature and the Arts, Preparation for the High School Equivalency Examination.*

1 ① ② ③ ④ ⑤	11 ① ② ③ ④ ⑤	21 ① ② ③ ④ ⑤	31 ① ② ③ ④ ⑤
2 ① ② ③ ④ ⑤	12 ① ② ③ ④ ⑤	22 ① ② ③ ④ ⑤	32 ① ② ③ ④ ⑤
3 ① ② ③ ④ ⑤	13 ① ② ③ ④ ⑤	23 ① ② ③ ④ ⑤	33 ① ② ③ ④ ⑤
4 ① ② ③ ④ ⑤	14 ① ② ③ ④ ⑤	24 ① ② ③ ④ ⑤	34 ① ② ③ ④ ⑤
5 ① ② ③ ④ ⑤	15 ① ② ③ ④ ⑤	25 ① ② ③ ④ ⑤	35 ① ② ③ ④ ⑤
6 ① ② ③ ④ ⑤	16 ① ② ③ ④ ⑤	26 ① ② ③ ④ ⑤	36 ① ② ③ ④ ⑤
7 ① ② ③ ④ ⑤	17 ① ② ③ ④ ⑤	27 ① ② ③ ④ ⑤	37 ① ② ③ ④ ⑤
8 ① ② ③ ④ ⑤	18 ① ② ③ ④ ⑤	28 ① ② ③ ④ ⑤	38 ① ② ③ ④ ⑤
9 ① ② ③ ④ ⑤	19 ① ② ③ ④ ⑤	29 ① ② ③ ④ ⑤	39 ① ② ③ ④ ⑤
10 ① ② ③ ④ ⑤	20 ① ② ③ ④ ⑤	30 ① ② ③ ④ ⑤	40 ① ② ③ ④ ⑤

Questions 1–4 refer to the following passage.

Statistics form the spine of the legend of Babe Didrikson Zaharias. This is true of nearly all athletes: the results of sporting events are finite
5 [measurable], almost never abstract. In most other human pursuits, in art, music, literature, and so forth, greatness is a matter of intangibles. But in sports there are winners and losers; the results
10 are unmistakable; the statistics are immutable [unchangeable]. In the case of Babe, the statistics that define her greatness are so impressive they seem almost too good to be true.

15 Between 1930 and 1932 she held American, Olympic, or world records in five different track and field events. During the A.A.U. national meet of 1932, she entered as the sole member of the
20 Golden Cyclones, a team sponsored by the Employers Casualty Company of Dallas; Babe scored thirty points in the meet. The next best team, the Illinois Women's Athletic Club, had twenty-two
25 members who scored a total of twenty-two points.

In the Olympics at Los Angeles, she won gold medals and set world records in the 80-meter hurdles and the javelin—
30 breaking the javelin record by an astounding eleven feet. She tied for first place in the high jump, setting another world record; officials ruled, however, that she had dived illegally during her
35 last successful jump and she was awarded the silver medal instead of the gold.

—Excerpted from *Whatta Gal: The Babe Didrickson Story*, by William O. Johnson and Nancy P. Williamson

1. What is the best title for this passage?
   (1) The Los Angeles Olympics
   (2) Babe Didrikson's Greatest Accomplishment
   (3) Sexism in Sports
   (4) Babe Didrikson: Star Athlete
   (5) Famous Female Athletes

2. The word *intangibles* (line 8) refers to things that
   (1) can be easily measured
   (2) cannot clearly be perceived or identified
   (3) people should not believe
   (4) involve mistakes
   (5) involve financial sacrifice

3. In the high jump at the Los Angeles Olympics, why did Babe Didrikson win a silver medal instead of a gold?
   (1) She had the second-highest jump in the event.
   (2) She broke a world record.
   (3) The officials ruled that she had dived illegally.
   (4) She could not break the record of 11 feet.
   (5) She failed in her final jump.

4. With which of the following statements would the author of this passage most likely agree?
   (1) Sports are more important than arts and literature.
   (2) The results of sporting events are often misunderstood.
   (3) Statistics alone do not tell the story of Babe Didrikson.
   (4) Greatness is easier to measure in sports than in the arts.
   (5) It is easier to excel in the arts than in athletics.

Questions 5–8 refer to the following passage.

He stopped the car and studied the opening with his field glasses. Then he motioned to the driver to go on and the car moved slowly along, the driver
5 avoiding wart-hog holes and driving around the mud castles ants had built. Then, looking across the opening, Wilson suddenly turned and said,

"By God, there they are!"

10 And looking where he pointed, while the car jumped forward and Wilson spoke in rapid Swahili to the driver, Macomber saw three huge, black animals looking almost cylindrical in
15 their long heaviness, like big black tank cars, moving at a gallop across the far edge of the open prairie. They moved at a stiff-necked, stiff-bodied gallop and he could see the upswept wide black horns
20 on their heads as they galloped heads out; the heads not moving.

"They're three old bulls," Wilson said. "We'll cut them off before they get to the swamp."

—Excerpted from "The Short Happy Life of Francis Macomber," by Ernest Hemingway

5. What does Wilson see across the open field?

(1) black tank cars
(2) another car and driver
(3) three bulls
(4) three cylinders
(5) a jumble of mud castles

6. How many people can you assume are in the car?

(1) only one
(2) two
(3) at least three
(4) four
(5) six

7. What kind of language is used in lines 13–16?

(1) literal
(2) persuasive
(3) informative
(4) descriptive
(5) informal

8. You can infer from the passage that Wilson and Macomber are

(1) visiting an urban zoo
(2) working on a cattle farm
(3) on safari in Africa
(4) trying to escape from dangerous bulls
(5) touring Europe

POST-TEST

Questions 9–11 refer to the following passage.

ColdAir AIR-CONDITIONER

WARRANTY

This warranty fully covers repair or replacement of your ColdAir air-conditioning unit for 90 days from date of purchase. ColdAir, Inc. shall determine whether an individual unit warrants repair or replacement at company expense. This warranty expires after 90 days from date of purchase. Thereafter, a limited warranty takes effect.

The limited warranty remains in force for a period of nine months from its effective date. It fully covers any adjustment or repair made necessary by defects in materials or workmanship.

If your ColdAir air-conditioner should require service, write to the address below for the name and address of an authorized service center near you.

Name _____

Address _____

City _____ State _____ Zip _____

Serial number of your ColdAir air-conditioning unit _____

To help us maintain up-to-date records on the warranty status of every product we sell, please complete this card and mail to:

ColdAir, Inc.

1000 River Road

Riceland, NY 10000

9. If you buy a ColdAir unit, how much time do you have to return it to the company for defects in workmanship?
   (1) 90 days
   (2) nine months
   (3) 30 days
   (4) one year
   (5) one year and three months

10. After seven months, the warranty in force will cover
    (1) replacement of a unit damaged by flood
    (2) repair to a unit damaged by flood
    (3) replacement of a unit that was stolen
    (4) replacement of a unit with faulty wiring
    (5) repair of a unit with a defective ventilation system

11. What should a customer do if a ColdAir unit fails after three months from date of purchase?
    (1) Buy a new unit since repairs are no longer covered.
    (2) Ship the unit back to the company facility in Riceland, NY.
    (3) Contact the Riceland facility for the name and address of a nearby service center.
    (4) Consult the Yellow Pages for the company's nearest service center.
    (5) Have the unit repaired locally and send the bill to ColdAir for reimbursement.

Questions 12–15 refer to the following passage.

"Where do they get vegetables like this?" Minnie asked. She saw other women feeling the tomatoes, sampling the lush bunches of grapes. "The prices
5   are the same as we pay, but what a difference."

Mrs. Jameson laughed a little. "It's worth driving over here, isn't it?" she said. "We used to live not far from here.
10 That's how I happen to know about it." But Mariana suspected this store was not unique, that in the gringo neighborhoods everything was a little better.

15 At the meat counter, Minnie was even more impressed. She examined carefully all the meat behind the glass, and then asked the butcher to cut some filet mignon. Mariana couldn't ever
20 recall hearing her mother order that, and she noticed it was the most expensive meat. She thought she understood why her mother ordered it.

25 On the way back to East Los Angeles, Mariana sensed her mother felt defensive and perhaps a little offended because the gringa had shown her a better way to do
30 something, had shown that shopping near home was not good enough for someone with taste.

She heard her mother say, "Next week Pete's buying me a new Cadillac.
35 Then I'll take you shopping with me," and Mariana had never seen such a forced smile on her mother's face.

"Oh, that'll be nice," Mrs. Jameson said.

—Excerpted from *Chicano*, by Richard Vasquez

12. Mariana is Minnie's
   (1) friend
   (2) daughter
   (3) mother
   (4) neighbor
   (5) aunt

13. It can be inferred that the store the women visited together is
   (1) located in Minnie's neighborhood
   (2) where Minnie usually shops
   (3) part of a discount food chain
   (4) located a distance from Minnie's neighborhood
   (5) owned by the Jameson family

14. Why might Minnie feel defensive and a little offended (lines 27–28)?
   (1) She had to travel a long way to buy the same food she could buy at home.
   (2) She discovered that the food sold in her neighborhood was inferior by comparison.
   (3) She could not afford to shop in fancy grocery stores.
   (4) Mrs. Jameson insulted her.
   (5) Mrs. Jameson misinformed her.

15. You can infer that Minnie ordered filet mignon because
   (1) she wanted to impress Mrs. Jameson
   (2) it was her husband's favorite food
   (3) she always liked to try new things
   (4) it was much cheaper than at her regular market
   (5) Mariana recommended it

Questions 16–20 refer to the following poem.

I'm Just a Stranger Here, Heaven Is My Home

The first sign was your hair,
unstraightened, shortened from worry,
and it had only been a year since the
wedding,
5   but you had grown older, Mama.
I felt your usual care
in the mustard greens, sweet potatoes
and chicken,
yet you smelled of whiskey and prayer.
10 I showed you the pictures,
asked which ones you'd like remade
and watched you fidget, unable to see
them.
Raising your arm, you spoke of your
15 rheumatism,
it seems like life left your arm first,
like crumbs given to front yard robins.
Age and need, those simple weeds,
were gathering around and taking you
20 away.

—Carole Clemmons

16. The tone of this poem is
   (1) ironic
   (2) pleasant
   (3) sorrowful
   (4) humorous
   (5) angry

17. What is the main idea of this poem?
   (1) An elderly alcoholic woman is likely to neglect herself.
   (2) People with elderly parents should visit them regularly.
   (3) Mothers continue to act like mothers even after their children are all grown up.
   (4) Age and need have caused noticeable changes in Mama.
   (5) Elderly women tend to suffer from depression.

18. Line 16 suggests that
   (1) Mama will probably lose her arm before she dies
   (2) Mama's life has lost value
   (3) Mama's needs have lessened with age
   (4) Mama can live as simply as a little robin
   (5) Mama's health is steadily declining

19. The word *fidget* (line 12) means to
   (1) compare closely
   (2) move nervously
   (3) laugh loudly
   (4) look on with interest
   (5) speak quickly

20. To what does the phrase "those simple weeds" (line 18) refer?
   (1) the yard inhabited by robins
   (2) whiskey and prayer
   (3) Mama's life
   (4) age and need
   (5) rheumatism

Questions 21–25 refer to a passage from *The Glass Menagerie*, a play by Tennessee Williams. Laura, the main character, is extremely shy and very self-conscious about a brace that she wears on one leg. She spends most of her time caring for a collection of small glass figurines.

[*JIM lights a cigarette and leans indolently {lazily} back on his elbows smiling at* LAURA *with a warmth and charm which lights her inwardly with*
5 *altar candles {pleases her very much}. She remains by the table, picks up a piece from the glass menagerie collection, and turns it in her hands to cover her tumult {confusion}.*]

10   JIM: [*After several reflective puffs on his cigarette*] What have you done since high school?

[*She seems not to hear him.*]

Huh?

15   [LAURA *looks up.*]

I said what have you done since high school, Laura?

LAURA: Nothing much.

JIM: You must have been doing
20   something these six long years.

LAURA: Yes.

JIM: Well, then, such as what?

LAURA: I took a business course at
25   business college—

JIM: How did that work out?

LAURA: Well, not very—well—I had to drop out, it gave me— indigestion—

30   [*JIM laughs gently.*]

JIM: What are you doing now?

LAURA: I don't do anything—much. Oh, please don't think I sit around doing nothing! My glass
35   collection takes up a good deal of time. Glass is something you have to take good care of.

JIM: What did you say—about glass?

40   LAURA: Collection I said—I have one—[*She clears her throat and turns away again, acutely shy.*]

JIM: [*Abruptly*] You know what I
45   judge to be the trouble with you? Inferiority complex! . . . Yep—that's what I judge to be your principal trouble. A lack of confidence in yourself as a
50   person. You don't have the proper amount of faith in yourself. . . .For instance that clumping you thought was so awful in high school. You say
55   that you even dreaded to walk into class. You see what you did? You dropped out of school, you gave up an education because of a clump,
60   which as far as I know was practically non-existent! A little physical defect is what you have. Hardly noticeable even! Magnified thousands of times
65   by imagination! You know what my strong advice to you is? Think of yourself as superior in some way!

21. What has Laura been doing since high school?

    (1) caring for her collection of little glass statues
    (2) working toward her business degree
    (3) keeping house for Jim and raising their children
    (4) volunteering at a school
    (5) undergoing therapy for an inferiority complex

22. Why does Laura pick up a glass figurine (lines 6–7)?

    (1) to prevent Jim from breaking it
    (2) to show Jim how fragile it is
    (3) because she is nervous and confused
    (4) because she is angry
    (5) because Jim's smoking irritates her

23. The dashes in lines 27–29 and 40–41 indicate that Laura

    (1) stutters
    (2) is afraid that Jim will make fun of her glass collection
    (3) has trouble sharing her thoughts with others
    (4) is confined indoors with a serious medical condition
    (5) is suffering another bout of indigestion

24. When Jim says Laura gave up an education "because of a clump" that was "practically non-existent," what does he mean?

    (1) Laura left school to tend a small garden.
    (2) Laura didn't have to wear her brace all the time.
    (3) Laura was self-conscious about a handicap that others hardly noticed.
    (4) Laura's brace was noisy.
    (5) Most of Laura's classmates ignored her.

25. Which of the following conclusions can you draw from this passage?

    (1) Women are more likely than men to have an inferiority complex.
    (2) Shyness is a sign of an inferiority complex.
    (3) An inferiority complex is a sign of shyness.
    (4) Someone who feels inferior probably is inferior.
    (5) An inferiority complex is a lack of self-confidence.

Questions 26–29 refer to the following review.

Playwright A. R. Gurney calls *Later Life* a comedy, and it has the witty dialogue to live up to the billing. But at its heart, this story of a man in
5 his middle years who can't bring himself to seize one last chance at happiness is no laughing matter.

If the play is to succeed, the audience had better feel for the
10 anguished Austin, a Boston Brahmin so caught in the spiderweb of his bloodline and upbringing that he can't let the free-spirited Ruth into his life even the second time around.

15 Regrettably, Northlight Theater's production of the work . . . does not achieve the desired effect. . . .

The story unfolds on an apartment building terrace overlooking Boston
20 Harbor. Inside, a party is going on, but outside, Austin and Ruth are becoming reacquainted.

They met years ago on Capri. He was a young naval officer fresh out of
25 Harvard; she was vacationing with friends from Southern Illinois University. The attraction was mutual and

instantaneous, but after one idyllic
afternoon, Austin walked away from the
30 relationship.

They both have gone on to
marriages, but at the time of their
second meeting, he is divorced and she
is separated. They could help each
35 other, but Austin again is incapable of
pressing forward. At the play's end, his
life is effectively over, and Ruth's
prospects are not much better.

Kristine Thatcher . . . captures
40 Ruth's resilience, warmth and zest for
life. It is easy to understand why
everyone at the party is rooting for
Austin to nab her.

Michael Gross . . . has the tougher
45 assignment. He must make the aloof
Austin not only understandable but
sympathetic, but the actor never reveals
what is going on beneath the seemingly
smooth surface.

50 Linda Kimbrough and Greg Vinkler,
however, are convincing and terrifically
comical in multiple roles as insensitive
party guests who wander onto the
terrace, interrupting the couple's
55 conversation.

—Excerpted from a review of *Later
Life*, by Virginia Gerst, *Skokie
Review,* October 6, 1994

26. What is the subject of this review?
   (1) a struggling regional theater
      company
   (2) the Northlight Theater's production
      of *Later Life*
   (3) the playwright A. R. Gurney
   (4) a made-for-television comedy
   (5) a romantic film

27. The character of Austin is best
   described as
   (1) free-spirited
   (2) snobbish
   (3) warm
   (4) sympathetic
   (5) dignified

28. With which of the following would the
   reviewer most likely agree?
   (1) Kristine Thatcher is miscast in the
      role of Ruth.
   (2) Michael Gross delivers a complex,
      sensitive portrait of Austin.
   (3) The character of Austin is poorly
      written.
   (4) The supporting actors turn in
      splendid performances.
   (5) The overall quality of the acting
      rescues a mediocre script.

29. The ending of *Later Life* can best be
   characterized as
   (1) bittersweet
   (2) joyful
   (3) satisfying
   (4) hopeful
   (5) surprising

Questions 30–33 refer to the following passage.

It was June and long past time for buying the special shoes that were quiet as a summer rain falling on the walks. . . . The grass was still pouring in
5 from the country, surrounding the sidewalks, stranding the houses. Any moment the town would capsize, go down and leave not a stir in the clover and weeds. And here Douglas stood,
10 trapped on the dead cement and the red-brick streets, hardly able to move.

"Dad!" He blurted it out. "Back there in that window, those Cream-Sponge Para Litefoot Shoes . . ."

15 His father didn't even turn. "Suppose you tell me why you need a new pair of sneakers. Can you do that?"

"Well . . ."

It was because they felt the way it
20 feels every summer when you take off your shoes for the first time and run in the grass. They felt like it feels sticking your feet out of the hot covers in wintertime to let the cold wind from the
25 open window blow on them suddenly and you let them stay out a long time until you pull them back in under the covers again to feel them, like packed snow. The tennis shoes felt like it
30 always feels the first time every year wading in the slow waters of the creek and seeing your feet below, half an inch further downstream, with refraction, than the real part of you above water.

35 "Dad," said Douglas, "it's hard to explain."

—Excerpted from *Dandelion Wine*, by Ray Bradbury

30. Which statement best expresses the main idea of the passage?

(1) Douglas wants to run and be free.
(2) The coming of summer worries Douglas.
(3) New sneakers would help Douglas experience the joy of summer.
(4) Douglas needs orthopedic sneakers for hiking in the back country.
(5) Douglas is a summer athlete.

31. The style of the paragraph beginning "It was because" is best described as

(1) informative
(2) persuasive
(3) descriptive
(4) formal
(5) sequential

32. It can be inferred that Douglas and his father are speaking as they walk along a

(1) wooded path
(2) mountain trail
(3) country road on the outskirts of town
(4) sidewalk in town
(5) beach

33. Why is it hard for Douglas to explain his desire for new sneakers?

(1) His father is uncaring.
(2) Some feelings are just hard for him to put into words.
(3) Douglas knows his family cannot afford to buy luxuries.
(4) Douglas is afraid of his father.
(5) There's nothing wrong with his old sneakers.

Questions 34–37 refer to the following passage from a newspaper story.

Sinatra before Swing
Early material reveals quieter side of the star

To most listeners today, he's the singer who crooned his way to stardom singing "My Kind of Town," "New York, New York," The Lady Is a Tramp" and "I
5 Get a Kick Out of You."

To most listeners, he's all about swagger and strut, the perennial tough guy in a tux, a shot glass in one hand, a microphone and a smoldering cigarette
10 in the other, the enduring symbol of an era when swing still was king.

Peel away the mythology, however; look past the high-life facade [surface] and the hard-edged repertoire [body of
15 work], and you'll find the Frank Sinatra that most of the world doesn't know, or doesn't want to.

Listen past his biggest hits, the anthems that every audience demands,
20 and you'll hear facets of Sinatra's music that shatter universally held perceptions.

It's that repertoire [mixture of songs]—brooding ballads, songs of
25 alienation [separation] and loss, aching love poems, tunes that Sinatra sang before he became a swinger, and long after—that finally is coming to light in a series of long-awaited releases and rare
30 reissues.

Much of this material hasn't been heard in 25 years or more; some of it never has been released before.

—Excerpted from a review by Howard Reich, *Chicago Tribune*

34. The subject of this passage is
   (1) the era of swing
   (2) new releases and rare reissues of Frank Sinatra's music
   (3) Frank Sinatra's tough-guy image
   (4) audience perceptions of Frank Sinatra
   (5) changing tastes in popular music

35. You can infer that "My Kind of Town" and "New York, New York" are examples of
   (1) brooding ballads
   (2) songs of loss
   (3) aching love poems
   (4) the kinds of songs usually identified with Frank Sinatra
   (5) the writer's favorite type of music

36. The writer suggests that the "long-awaited releases and rare reissues" (lines 29–30) reveal
   (1) why Frank Sinatra was viewed as a symbol of swing
   (2) a softer side to Sinatra's music
   (3) the singer's best-known repertoire
   (4) the reasons for his popularity
   (5) a familiar aspect of Sinatra's musical style

37. *Mythology* (line 12) refers to
   (1) Frank Sinatra's image as a tough guy living the high life
   (2) songs that audiences demand
   (3) Sinatra's biggest hits
   (4) the way that ordinary people look up to celebrities
   (5) music that shatters common perceptions

Questions 38–40 refer to the following excerpt from an index to a cookbook.

INDEX

Onion recipes, cont'd.
    Rita's Sour-Sweet Meatballs, 81
    Sausage Stuffing for Turkey, 339
    Shrimp Bake, 187
    Spaghetti Casserole, 304
    Spaghetti Meat Sauce, 269
    Tacos, Meat Filling, 281
    Tuna Noodle Casserole, 197
Orange recipes
    Cheesecake, 235
    Marmalade Glaze, 160
    Sauce, 358
Oriental Sweet-Sour Pork, 296
Oven-Fried Chicken, 342
Oven-Fried Fish, 342
Packaging foods for freezer, 31
    aluminum containers or foil, 33
    plastic containers, 34
    Saran Wrap, 34
    waxed paper, 33
Pancake recipes
    Apple, 132
    Blueberry, 124
    Nut, 124
    Pineapple, 124
Parmesian, Veal, 294
Parsley Carrots, 378
Pasta recipes
    Lasagne Casserole, 278
    Macaroni and Ham, 303
    Macaroni, Cheese, and Tomato
      Casserole, 403
      with Ground Beef, 404
    Noodle Nests, 406
    Rita's Noodle Ring, 405
    Spaghetti Casserole, 304
    Spaghetti Meat Sauce, 269
    Two-Layer Italian Macaroni, 404

---

38. On which page would you find a recipe for nut pancakes?

  (1) 22
  (2) 51
  (3) 125
  (4) 124
  (5) 126

39. Which of the following sets of pasta recipes can be found on the same page?

  (1) Lasagna Casserole and Macaroni and Ham
  (2) Lasagna Casserole and Spaghetti Meat Sauce
  (3) Two-layer Italian Macaroni and Macaroni, Cheese, and Tomato Casserole with Ground Beef
  (4) Spaghetti Casserole and Rita's Noodle Ring
  (5) Noodle Nests and Macaroni and Ham

40. Which pages tell you whether to freeze oven-fried chicken in waxed paper or in Saran Wrap?

  (1) 342
  (2) 31
  (3) 34 and 35
  (4) 342 and 34
  (5) 33 and 34

1. **(4)** This passage focuses on Babe Didrikson's star performances in different sporting events. At best, the other choices are only partially correct.

2. **(2)** Lines 4–5 state that the results in sports are finite and almost never abstract. The author contrasts this with art, music, and literature. *Intangibles*, therefore, are things that are abstract or beyond human measurement.

3. **(3)** Although Babe Didrikson tied for the highest jump, she was awarded second place because officials ruled that she had dived illegally.

4. **(4)** The first paragraph says that in the arts, literature, and music, "greatness is a matter of intangibles" but that, in sports, statistics define greatness.

5. **(3)** This is stated in the last paragraph.

6. **(3)** You can count three people in the car: Wilson, Macomber, and the driver. Therefore, you can assume that there are at least three people.

7. **(4)** The author says the animals looked "like big black tank cars" and "almost cylindrical." These are examples of vividly descriptive language.

8. **(3)** You can infer that Wilson and Macomber are driving somewhere in the great outdoors. They are most probably in Africa, since Swahili is an African language.

9. **(4)** The warranty on the air conditioner provides full coverage for three months (90 days) and limited coverage for nine additional months. Three months plus nine months equal twelve months, or one year.

10. **(5)** The limited warranty would be in force at this time, and it covers only repairs made necessary by defects in material or workmanship. It does not cover replacements.

11. **(3)** The warranty instructs customers who need service to write to the company for the location of the nearest service center.

12. **(2)** Mariana uses the word *mother* in the third paragraph when she thinks about Minnie. This tells you that she must be Minnie's daughter.

13. **(4)** Since the women had to drive a distance, and Minnie is surprised by what she sees, you can infer that the store is not in Minnie's neighborhood.

14. **(2)** Mrs. Jameson had shown her a store much bigger and better than the markets in Minnie's neighborhood.

15. **(1)** Minnie wanted Mrs. Jameson to think that she wasn't dazzled by the beautiful store and that buying expensive items was as natural for her as for the "gringa."

16. **(3)** The poet is obviously saddened by her mother's failing condition.

17. **(4)** The poet sees how much her mother has declined from age and need.

18. **(5)** The poet says that "life left your arm first," meaning that Mama's health is continuing to weaken. *First* implies more to come.

19. **(2)** This is the best choice in this context.

20. **(4)** You can infer that age and need are "those simple weeds" collecting around Mama.

21. **(1)** Laura tells Jim that her "glass collection takes up a good deal of time" (lines 34–36).

22. **(3)** The stage directions tell you that Laura turns the figurine in her hands "to cover her tumult." You can infer that this is also part of the reason she picked it up.

23. **(3)** Dashes indicate interruptions. Laura is interrupting herself because she is unsure of herself and unable to express her thoughts.

24. (3) Something that is "practically non-existent" is noticed very little or not at all.

25. (5) Jim says, "Inferiority complex! . . . Yep— that's what I judge to be your principal trouble. A lack of confidence in yourself as a person" (lines 46–50).

26. (2) The first paragraph identifies the play. The third paragraph names the theater company.

27. (2) You can infer that Austin is snobbish from the description of him as a "Boston Brahmin so caught in the spiderweb of his bloodline and upbringing. . . ."

28. (4) The last paragraph praises the supporting cast as "convincing and terrifically comical."

29. (1) The sixth paragraph says that at the end of the play, Austin's life "is effectively over, and Ruth's prospects are not much better."

30. (3) The main idea is the connection Douglas makes between new sneakers and his anticipated enjoyment of summer.

31. (3) This paragraph describes in great emotional detail Douglas's feelings about summertime.

32. (4) Line 11 refers to paved streets. "Back there in that window" (lines 12–13) suggests a storefront, which would most likely be in town.

33. (2) Most of the passage is about what new sneakers feel like to Douglas and what they mean to him. But his response to his father shows that he doesn't know how exactly to explain these feelings or translate them into a practical argument for getting new shoes.

34. (2) This information is given in the last two paragraphs.

35. (4) The first paragraph identifies such songs as the kind of music "most listeners" associate with Frank Sinatra.

36. (2) The fifth paragraph identifies the newly released material as a collection of ballads and other sad songs. These suggest a softer side to the singer's work.

37. (1) Since the mythology can be peeled back, it must be on the outside. Sinatra, on the surface, has long had the image of a tough character leading a wild life in the fast lane.

38. (4) Under "Pancake recipes," find the sub-heading "Nut."

39. (3) Look under "Pasta recipes." Only two pasta recipes appear on the same page.

40. (5) Under "Oven-Fried Chicken," you will find only a recipe. If you look under "Packaging foods for freezer," you can find Saran Wrap on page 34 and waxed paper on page 33.

Post-Test Evaluation Chart

Use the chart below to help you identify any areas in which you need additional practice. Circle the number of any questions you answered incorrectly. Then note the corresponding skill and content areas. Read across the rows for content areas and down the columns for skills. If your mistakes cluster in any one row or column, it means that you need more work in that particular area.

Skill Area/ Content Area	Literal Comprehension	Inferential Comprehension	Analysis	Application
Nonfiction Prose (pages 69–87)	3, 9	1, 2, 4	10, 39	11, 38, 40
Prose Fiction (pages 89–119)	5, 12	6, 8, 13, 15, 32	14, 30, 33	7, 31
Poetry (pages 121–139)	19	18, 20	17	16
Drama (pages 141–153)	21	22, 24	25	23
Commentaries on the Arts (pages 155–183)	26, 34, 37	27, 35	28, 36	29

Answer Key

CHAPTER 1
LITERAL UNDERSTANDING

EXERCISE 1
Pages 22–23

1. **Paragraph 1:** (d)
   Paragraph 2: (c)
   Paragraph 3: (a)
   Paragraph 4: (b)
2. **(3)** From the second paragraph on, the passage focuses on opportunities for adults.
3. **(2)** The passage provides information about adults returning to college.

EXERCISE 2
Page 25

1. 1832. This is stated in the second sentence of the second paragraph.
2. He believed the chiefs had been tricked into giving up the land. This information is provided in the last sentence of the first paragraph.
3. He refused to surrender the land. This is explained in the first two sentences.
4. Indian tribes of Illinois. This information is found in the first paragraph.
5. He was sent to a reservation at Fort Des Moines. This is stated in the last sentence of the second paragraph.

EXERCISE 3
Page 27

1. To equivocate means to use unclear language either to mislead someone or to avoid committing oneself to a particular position. The key words *instead of* point to the opposite of *straightforward*.
2. A flashback is an intense, emotional memory of a past time or event. The meaning is given after the key word *or*.
3. A surrogate is a substitute. The key words *that is* point to the meaning.
4. To have charisma means to have extraordinary powers. The word is defined by the sentence directly following it.
5. *Modular* refers to self-contained parts—in this case, computer parts. The comma introduces the definition.

6. A proverb is an old, popular saying that expresses a well-known truth or bit of wisdom. The key word *yet* signals the explanation.
7. A bellwether is a leader. The definition is given in the second sentence.
8. A quarantine is an enforced period of isolation to prevent the spread of disease. The key word *means* points to the definition.

PRE-GED PRACTICE
EXERCISE 4
Pages 28–31

1. **(2)** The passage traces the history of New Mexico from prehistoric times to the present. The phrase "the memory of New Mexico's fiery past" indicates that the subject of the discussion is history.
2. **(5)** The second paragraph specifically says that the Spanish arrived after the Apaches and Navahos.
3. **(3)** The second paragraph states that Coronado was "compelled by rumors of gold."
4. **(2)** The first paragraph defines ristras as "strands of blazing red chili peppers, hung from ranch house porches."
5. **(1)** The paragraph is about the start of the modern era, which began when the railroad came in.
6. **(3)** See the last paragraph. A hamlet is a small settlement essentially unchanged by time.
7. **(1)** The last paragraph describes the air in Lamy as fresh and clean in 1880 and still today.
8. **(4)** Lines 8–9 tell you that prehistoric hunters came to New Mexico as long as 11,500 years ago.
9. **(2)** Washington persuaded his mother to get him a book.
10. **(2)** The passage is about the author's first experiences with reading.
11. **(4)** The author expresses no opinion about his stepfather's job or about the kind of job he himself would one day like to have.
12. **(2)** When he moved with his family to a new cabin in West Virginia, he persuaded his mother to get him a book to learn from.
13. **(1)** Washington's mother *procured*, or *got possession of*, an old spelling book for him.
14. **(3)** Washington *devoured*, or *enjoyed greatly*, the spelling book his mother gave him.
15. **(4)** The number "18" is an identification number that is marked on the barrels his stepfather packs.

CHAPTER 2
MAKING INFERENCES

EXERCISE 1
Page 35

1. **(1)** This is not stated, but it is the best summary of all the details in the passage.
2. **(2)** He continues despite his great surprise.
3. **(3)** It is a sign of their courage that they continue toward the strange planet.

PRE-GED PRACTICE
EXERCISE 2
Pages 36–37

1. **(3)** Paul is probably older, because his children are much older than Tom's.
2. **(1)** Paul ends the conversation by saying he must return to his office. Of all the answer choices, an insurance salesman is most likely to work out of an office.
3. **(5)** The whole conversation is about Tom's divorce; he has had the "worst day" of his life and "split for good."
4. **(2)** Paul's advice is to try kindness. Tom won't hear of it. "Impossible," he says.
5. **(5)** Tom describes his job as a "dead-end job."
6. **(3)** The term *alimony* refers to the payments Tom must make to his ex-wife after the divorce.

EXERCISE 3
Page 39

1. in the newspaper, according to the second paragraph
2. in magazines and on television, according to the last sentence of the second paragraph
3. direct mail
4. twenty cents, according to the chart

EXERCISE 4
Page 40

1. **(2)** The coupon may be used for a discount on an item costing $15 or more.
2. **(3)** There is a limit of one coupon per item, so two coupons would be needed.
3. **(3)** The small print at the bottom of the coupon says it is not for use with sale items.

PRE-GED PRACTICE
EXERCISE 5
Page 41

1. **(2)** Since the Mendenhall method uses recycled asphalt, asphalt suppliers stand to lose business to it.

2. **(5)** The author describes the test process enthusiastically, referring to a "lovely reborn lane" produced with "scarcely a dollar . . . spent for new asphalt."
3. **(1)** The process is economical in that it uses less time and little or no new asphalt.
4. **(4)** The new asphalt was produced from the old. The second paragraph describes how the old pavement was softened and repoured into the roadway.

EXERCISE 6
Page 42

1. Blend in the chocolate and vanilla.
2. Four. Since one pie calls for two eggs, two pies would require four.
3. Pour the mixture into a pastry shell and chill it.
4. One stick of margarine equals one-half cup.

EXERCISE 7
Page 43

1. **T** The entire passage is about the Great Depression.
2. **F** The passage is not critical. Its purpose is simply to provide information.
3. **T** The last sentence in the second paragraph says that Roosevelt's reforms "helped ease the depression."
4. **T** The last paragraph gives several examples of the long-term effects of the depression.

PRE-GED PRACTICE
EXERCISE 8
Pages 44–45

1. **(3)** The author merely guesses that the doctor was from India, whereas she directly states in her first paragraph that the doctor had a thick accent.
2. **(5)** The entire passage, and particularly the last paragraph, is about the young woman's confusion and upset.
3. **(5)** The young woman is a sympathetic character, and the events of the story are told from her point of view.
4. **(4)** From the events mentioned in lines 12–14, you can infer that Sue grew up quickly at age 15.
5. **(3)** Lines 16–17 tell you that Sue moved back with her mother after Sue and Larry had a fight.
6. **(5)** The passage doesn't say why Larry left town. Sue assumes Larry left because of her pregnancy, but she's not sure.

ANSWER KEY

CHAPTER 3
ANALYZING LITERATURE
AND THE ARTS IDEAS

EXERCISE 1
Page 48

1. **(2)** The eating binge at the bakery is the focal point of the passage. All of the events in the story build toward it. It ends not only the passage but also Vana's diet.
2. **(1)** The details are presented from the least important to the most important, culminating in Vana's eventual surrender to sweets.

EXERCISE 2
Page 50

1. 2, 1, 4, 3, 5
2. **(1)** Jake should probably secure his remaining food and supplies before deciding what to do next.

EXERCISE 3
Page 52

1. **T** The second paragraph discusses in detail the limitations of Norberto's formal schooling.
2. **F** Carmen never saw the reading specialist. She helped Norberto because she wanted to and because he was agreeable.

EXERCISE 4
Page 54

1. Both were originally from the same neighborhood, former basketball stars, and Vietnam veterans.
2. The last paragraph mentions they each promise better jobs, schools, roads, and lives for citizens in the district.
3. John is a wealthy Republican backed by professionals, white-collar workers, farmers, and businesspeople. Peter is a steelworker and a Democrat closely identified with labor and minorities.

PRE-GED PRACTICE
EXERCISE 5
Page 56

1. **(3)** The globe is grouped with educational items. In the third paragraph, the author says, "Never one to neglect his schooling, my sleepyhead cuddled up to his world globe. . . ."
2. **(4)** The last paragraph places the dirty sock in the mixed category.
3. **(1)** The second paragraph lists batteries with the toys.

EXERCISE 6
Page 58

1. **(3)** Sentence fragments and the exclamation *Whoa* are characteristics of informal speech. Merely talking to oneself is informal.
2. **(2)** Cheri becomes increasingly tense and rattled by the sequence of frightening events and disturbing coincidences.

EXERCISE 7
Page 59

1. Formal. This passage uses more difficult words and larger sentences than would be used in an informal passage.
2. Forceful. The speaker presents the message in a vigorous, confident manner.

EXERCISE 8
Pages 60–61

1. **(1)** The books are listed alphabetically by author.
2. **(1)** Rountree's book, *On Women Turning 50,* presents profiles of 18 women over the age of 50.
3. **(2)** Friedan's *The Fountain of Age* was published in 1993, and so was Rountree's book, *On Women Turning 50.* Although 1994 is one of the choices given, none of the books listed was published in that year.
4. **(2)** From the title and short description, Berman's book, with its inspirational essays, would have the most comfort to offer a person struggling with fear of aging.
5. **(3)** *The Golden Years: Fit for Life* gives tips on exercise and finances.

EXERCISE 9
Page 62

1. **F** The passage is about a military figure, but there is nothing military about the writing style, which is somewhat formal.
2. **F** The passage does not criticize any persons or events. It is simply informative, in a literary way.
3. **T** Elizabeth's skirt "billowed like a balloon, flew out in front, then lifted over her head" (line 6).
4. **T** The last sentence says that other women took up the practice of sewing lead bars into their skirt hems.
5. **T** This is the subject of the whole passage.
6. **T** In line 10, Mrs. Custer is described as taking constitutionals about the post; line 5 mentions the walks she takes around the area.

7. F The passage states that Mrs. Custer's dresses are "five yards around."

8. F The passage says that "a dozen years later all were wearing bar lead in their skirt hems on the windy western plains."

PRE-GED PRACTICE
EXERCISE 10
Pages 63–65

1. **(1)** The first paragraph quotes Aunt Rosie directly about not letting the anger take over.

2. **(1)** Nothing in the passage indicates that Aunt Rosie pushes her way into situations where she is not wanted. The other choices are all reasonable inferences.

3. **(3)** The main idea is presented in the very first sentence. Inconsiderate behavior can certainly ruin a marriage, but it is not the main idea of this selection.

4. **(5)** This is most in keeping with Aunt Rosie's advice to keep anger under control and express one's true feelings in a calm fashion.

5. **(3)** This passage is written in an informal prose style.

6. **(4)** In the first paragraph, Aunt Rosie specifically says that nothing is solved by letting anger take over.

7. **(2)** The writer prevented a fight by following Aunt Rosie's advice. Instead of an angry outburst, she simply told her husband how she felt and why.

8. **(2)** Lines 13–14 describe Les as standing hesitantly, as if his wife might throw something. From this you can infer that he expected his wife to be angry.

9. **(4)** Lines 22–27 explain why Les came home late from work.

10. **(3)** The passage says that Les had to settle a change of plans with the foreman at a construction site and that he carried a briefcase. From this you can infer that Les may be an architect.

11. **(2)** Lines 15–17 describe Les as apologizing softly with tired eyes and his shoulders drooping. From this you can infer that he felt sorry and hesitant.

12. **(1)** The writer seems to be optimistic since things worked out better than expected with her husband. Part of this is due to a change in the writer's attitude about her husband's behavior.

CHAPTER 4
NONFICTION PROSE

EXERCISE 1
Page 70

1. **T** This is indicated in the first paragraph.
2. **T** This is stated in the third paragraph.
3. **F** No reference is made to other youth shelters.

4. **F** The subject of the piece is Covenant House.
5. **F** Scan the article for children's ages. The fourth paragraph mentions a child of 11.
6. **F** The second paragraph says, "No child is ever turned away."
7. **F** According to the second paragraph, Covenant House has 200 part-time workers.
8. **F** Sanctuary is safe haven. Troubled teens too rarely find sanctuary from the harsh world of the street.

EXERCISE 2
Page 71

1. Murder by arsenic poisoning. This is explained in the second and third paragraphs.
2. Sleepiness, insomnia, swollen feet, excessive weight gain. See the last sentence of the third paragraph.
3. The autopsy revealed an enlarged liver, a symptom of arsenic poisoning. This is stated in the second sentence of the third paragraph.
4. A well-preserved body in death. See the last paragraph.
5. He analyzed strands of Napoleon's hair. See the fourth paragraph.
6. On the island of St. Helena, to which he had been exiled. See the first and third paragraphs.

EXERCISE 3
Page 72

1. **F** The last paragraph says that a better basic understanding of these diseases is needed.
2. **F** NIAID's program calls for more scientific research into the disease processes. The third paragraph says that contact-tracing has been of only limited benefit.
3. **T** This is explained in the last paragraph.
4. **T** The first paragraph links complications to suffering, which implies negative effects.
5. **T** The third paragraph mentions new drug-resistant strains of disease.

EXERCISE 4
Page 74

1. **(2)** This is the theme of the entire passage.
2. **(1)** This is stated in the second sentence of the second paragraph.
3. **(2)** In the first sentence of the third paragraph, the author introduces his personal opinion with the words *I believe*.
4. **(1)** The last two sentences of the passage quote the graduate who has just been promoted.

EXERCISE 5
Page 76

1. **(3)** The first paragraph stresses the drawbacks of the other diets.
2. **(1)** *Anemic* and *homesick* are examples of biased language here. The other choices present information in neutral terms.

EXERCISE 6
Page 77

1. (b)
2. (c)
3. (d)
4. (a)
5. (e)
6. (f)
7. (g)

EXERCISE 7
Pages 78–79

1. **(3)** The purpose of any editorial is to persuade.
2. **(2)** The third paragraph quotes the constitutional "right of the people to keep and bear arms."
3. **(3)** Lines 16–19 tell why a ban on handguns will not solve the crime problem. The fourth paragraph explicitly mentions illegal gun sales, and the sixth paragraph protests a tax increase.
4. **(1)** The last two paragraphs support the writer's point of view about how defenseless law-abiding citizens would be without handguns.

EXERCISE 8
Pages 80–81

1. **(1)** This is plainly stated in the last sentence.
2. **(1)** The mention of an "angry husband" and the fact that a police officer was shot indicate that a fight took place.
3. **(2)** The editorial argues that violent crime declined in England after handguns were outlawed and implies that a ban here would have a similar effect.
4. **(3)** Both editorials urge increased protection against crime. They cannot agree on what real protection is or should be.

PRE-GED PRACTICE
EXERCISE 9
Pages 82–87

1. **(2)** The first paragraph suggests the title by mentioning the different groups present at the dedication. The article goes on to describe their respective concerns.
2. **(4)** This is a factual account written in the style of straight news.
3. **(3)** This is stated in the last paragraph.
4. **(2)** The passage discusses the many changes that electric technology has brought to people's lives.

5. **(4)** In this sentence, the phrase refers to a process of unconscious learning.
6. **(3)** Since electric technology implies the use of electricity, television is the correct answer.
7. **(5)** The statement that "the older training of observation has become quite irrelevant in this new time" (lines 34–36) implies that we must learn new ways of relating to today's technology.
8. **(1)** The second paragraph states that the Cornish miners introduced the Wisconsin miners to better methods of extracting ore, with the results that old mines were reopened and new ones were discovered.
9. **(1)** The subject of the passage is the history of mining in southwest Wisconsin. All of the information falls under this general topic.
10. **(3)** The last paragraph explains how, whenever market prices fell, hundreds of miners found themselves unemployed.
11. **(3)** The purpose is to salute the memory of two people whose joint legacy has enriched an entire community.
12. **(5)** The fourth paragraph states that Walter and Lavinia fell in love with the same idea. They shared a common vision and the will to realize it.
13. **(1)** A stereotype is a generalization. Lavinia Phelps did not conform to the stereotype, or common image, of an old woman quietly at home, no longer a productive member of her community.
14. **(2)** The language emphasizes Representative Palmer's wealth, ignorance, and obvious insensitivity to the farmers' plight.
15. **(2)** The third paragraph sharply contrasts the almost cartoonishly overdressed politician enjoying public attention with the many farmers who must go into debt just to keep their land.
16. **(5)** Representative Palmer's actions, words, and even her wardrobe are all calculated to draw attention from the press. Her only real goal is re-election. She shows no interest in farmers' problems, no understanding of them, and no desire to meet or hear from real voters with real concerns.
17. **(3)** *Festooned* means decorated.
18. **(2)** Palmer spoke first at Spring Agriculture Convention in Torrence.
19. **(3)** Palmer promised to seek more federal aid to agriculture (lines 24–25).

CHAPTER 5
PROSE FICTION

EXERCISE 1
Page 93

1. **(3)** The first sentence of the paragraph states that "he knew he must explore this island quickly." The last sentence of the first paragraph refers again to an island.
2. **(3)** The second paragraph mentions "midsummer shells." July is the only midsummer month listed in the choices.
3. **(1)** A bob-white is a bird. There is no evidence that Pentaquod is running away from anyone. From his name and the simile "eat like a chieftain," it can be inferred that he is an Indian.
4. **(1)** Pentaquod's observations of the surroundings reassure him that he will be able to provide for himself.
5. **(2)** The phrase "if he could but catch it" indicates the availability of food.

EXERCISE 2
Pages 98–99

1. **(3)** Johnny resents Mack. He talks back to him and won't cooperate. He describes the detective as fat and stupid. His behavior shows hostility.
2. **(1)** In these lines, Johnny is thinking things over. He expresses self-hatred and an urgent need to conceal his fear. These are evidence of a deep conflict within him.
3. **(2)** When Johnny learns of Eddie's death, he begins to doubt himself and becomes afraid. This is why he tries to escape.
4. **(1)** Clues that reveal the setting include the detective, the two cops at the door, the plainclothesman, and the female officer.
5. **(2)** Johnny's friend Eddie has been fatally stabbed. We know Johnny witnessed the stabbing because he says he knew Eddie was dead when the officers came to the door and because he regrets not having stayed away.

EXERCISE 3
Pages 100–101

1. **(1)** Although damage to the aircraft is mentioned, the action centers around the loss and restoration of oxygen in the cabin.

2. **(2)** The fourth paragraph states that Harris accepted the risk, which is another way of saying that he took a gamble. He gambled because he believed that the odds were worth the risk.
3. **(3)** The passengers were able to breathe again when the plane reached 12,000 feet and regained consciousness at 10,000 feet.
4. **(1)** The fourth paragraph mentions "further structural damage," implying that some damage was already done.
5. **(2)** This is the point toward which the action builds and from which it begins to resolve itself. The pilot risks possible destruction of the plane for a chance to restore oxygen to the passengers.

EXERCISE 4
Page 104

1. He felt faint. He was trying to keep himself from fainting.
2. He is determined. He forces away thoughts of weakness or failure.
3. Himself. He is encouraging and reassuring himself out loud. He tells himself, "You have to last." There is no sign that anyone else is in the boat with him.
4. The forward part of a boat. See line 7.

EXERCISE 5
Page 105

1. **D** The narrator felt, in turn, "nearly smothered," "squeezed," "cramped," and "perfectly miserable," which all make for an extremely uncomfortable trip.
2. **D** The adults did not speak to him except to complain or scold.
3. **A** The narrator is a child. He is seated between two men so he doesn't fall. The woman refers to his "young" bones.
4. **D** The boy is described in line 8 as having short legs.
5. **D** The woman was cruel. She poked him with her shoe and scolded him if he moved.

PRE-GED PRACTICE
EXERCISE 6
Pages 106–107

1. **(3)** A first-person narrator is telling the story. See lines 12 and 16.
2. **(2)** Boggs says, "Come out and meet the man you've swindled." To swindle means to cheat.
3. **(1)** Lines 36–38 describe Sherburn as "a heap the best dressed man in that town."
4. **(2)** This is stated in line 16.
5. **(2)** He threatens to come after Boggs if Boggs "opens his mouth against him" after one o'clock (lines 42–46).
6. **(3)** The townspeople yell at Boggs, laugh at him, and sass him. One of them says Boggs doesn't mean anything by his behavior and would never hurt anyone. All this adds up to a colorful but harmless character.
7. **(2)** The misspelling is deliberate. The author wants the reader to hear the regional speech.

EXERCISE 7
Page 109

1. (d)
2. (g)
3. (h)
4. (a)
5. (j)
6. (b)
7. (f)
8. (c)
9. (e)
10. (i)

EXERCISE 8
Page 110

1. **L**
2. **L**
3. **F** The expression refers to great happiness, not acrobatics.
4. **L**
5. **L**
6. **L**
7. **F** The world doesn't actually smile. The expression refers to happiness or good luck.
8. **F** The marriage was not literally made in heaven; it was a happy, promising union.
9. **F** People do not literally walk upon the air. But happiness is a feeling of joy mixed with lightness.
10. **F** The expression refers to great eagerness and impatience. People cannot physically be beside themselves.

EXERCISE 9
Pages 110–111

1. **(2)** The paragraph uses vivid figurative speech to describe tractors digging up the earth.
2. **(3)** Insects do not move at great speed or kick up huge clouds of dust. They crawl along the ground.
3. **(1)** The tractors are depicted as plowing through everything—fences, dooryards, hills, gulches, water courses, and houses—causing destruction.
4. **(1)** This is figurative language, transforming machines into the image of pigs.
5. **(2)** Line 10 describes the man as a "robot in the seat."

EXERCISE 10
Page 112

1. **(3)** The first sentence says that a moth flew into a candle. The rest of the paragraph is built around this event.
2. **(2)** To ignite means to catch fire. The moth's wings caught fire like tissue paper would have—extremely fast.
3. **(2)** Crackling and pistol fire are both sounds.
4. **(1)** "Green leaves" and "red trunk of a pine" (line 7) suggest a forest setting.

EXERCISE 11
Pages 114–115

1. **(2)** The first paragraph says Pete "could just see himself in a new home." The passage describes his experiences with real estate salesmen.
2. **(3)** The second paragraph says that Pete believed his financial success would enable him to live wherever he chose.
3. **(1)** Both men avoid answering Pete's questions or telling him the truth—that, because of his race, he is not welcome in the development. Their responses to Pete evade the point of his questions.
4. **(3)** Although Pete can afford to live where he wants, racial discrimination still keeps him out of this neighborhood.

PRE-GED PRACTICE
EXERCISE 12
Pages 116–119

1. **(5)** His feeling of being like an outsider is expressed in the first sentence of the third paragraph.

2. **(2)** The second paragraph describes how the narrator crossed over a fence to get to an area strewn with clothes and weapons and bodies under a hot sun. The third paragraph specifically refers to a battle ground.

3. **(4)** The image of such a machine is used to convey the inhumanity of war.

4. **(3)** The passage is about the pain and misery of war. Words such as "terrible," "grim," "littered with clothes and guns," "mournful company," "swollen forms," "agitated bodies," "blood-stained crowd," "cursing, groaning, and wailing" all show the agony of war.

5. **(3)** The whole passage is about Simple's long life of suffering.

6. **(1)** In the first paragraph, Simple speaks of having been "born young, black, voteless, poor, and hungry, in a state where white folks did not even put Negroes on the census." He resents having had to work so hard for so little in return.

7. **(4)** Simple lists the ways in which being black has led to his poverty and his hard life.

8. **(1)** The first several sentences show that this scene takes place in the kitchen at breakfast time.

9. **(4)** Although the young man jokes with his grandmother and won't give her a straight answer, he shows her genuine affection. He even tells her, "I'm nuts about you" (line 34).

10. **(2)** Her reference to a good night's sleep and her advice to avoid a chill show that she is concerned about her grandson's physical health.

11. **(5)** This is stated in line 41.

12. **(3)** Rain helps establish the gloomy mood.

13. **(1)** Yossarian is embittered and overwhelmed by the injustice and poverty he sees around him.

14. **(4)** The last line, "What a lousy earth!" sums up the passage. Yossarian takes a very negative, pessimistic view of the world.

CHAPTER 6
POETRY

EXERCISE 1
Page 123

1. **Stanza 1:** stair, care
   Stanza 2: smell, tell

Stanza 3: near, hear
Stanza 4: ago, know

2. **(3)** lonely older woman who lives alone (Reread the last line of each stanza.)

EXERCISE 2
Pages 126–127

1. **(1)** The author is sad that her mother missed out on so much of the beauty and gaiety in life. She also feels love and gratitude because her mother tried to give her something beautiful to hold on to.

2. **(2)** Lines 9 and 10 say, "My mother reached for beauty and for its lack she died."

3. **(2)** We do not know the mother's occupation, but line 4 says that "the tenement her orbit." The poem also mentions "the broken molding" (line 7) and the "filthy street" (line 8); so we know that she lived in a gloomy environment.

4. **(2)** The daughter remembers her mother as having tried to rise above their gloomy circumstances and reaching out for something better.

5. Answers will vary. Possible meaning: The duty and hard work of raising a child in the bleak environment of the tenement house simply overwhelmed the mother, despite her best efforts.

6. The rhyming words in lines 1 and 3 are *beauty* and *duty;* in lines 2 and 4, the words *died* and *pride* rhyme.

EXERCISE 3
Page 130

1. **S** Note the word *like*.
2. **M**
3. **M**
4. **S** Note the word *than* (two times).
5. **M**

EXERCISE 4
Page 131

1. ball of dark yarn
2. *gathers, loosens, spreads,* and *unravel*
3. fog and blue strands

PRE-GED PRACTICE
EXERCISE 5
Page 133

1. **(5)** The theme of the poem is the cramped, impersonal environment of a large apartment building.
2. **(3)** This simile uses the word *like* to compare people living in a large apartment building to bees swarming in a hive.
3. **(4)** *Comb* and *home* rhyme; the ending of each word sounds alike.
4. **(4)** The poet uses the words *identical* and *cramped* to describe the living spaces.

PRE-GED PRACTICE
EXERCISE 6
Page 134

1. **(1)** This comparison is made in lines 9 and 10, "stars are great drops of golden dew."
2. **(3)** This is a metaphor. A comparison is made without the use of the words *like, as,* or *than.*
3. **(3)** Music. The poet refers to a band playing and, twice, to singing.
4. **(5)** The poet is expressing the happiness of one who is in love. He uses the phrase *I love you* twice.

EXERCISE 7
Page 135

1. **(1)** Without using *like, as,* or *than,* the poet compares the crows' voices to thunder.
2. **(3)** Simile. In lines 1 and 2, crows "speak *like* men to one another."

PRE-GED PRACTICE
EXERCISE 8
Pages 136–139

1. **(2)** New York City. The last line says the bus has New York license plates.
2. **(3)** *Escapism* describes the poet's mood. The passenger seems angry and wants to escape from his urban surroundings.
3. **(3)** The driver is African American. In race-torn cities, the driver and passenger will switch places so that the bus will have an African-American passenger and a white driver.
4. **(4)** Lines 10 and 11 explain the passenger's need to show others that the driver has done well up North.
5. **(5)** The passenger wants to go to a small fishing village in an unknown part of Florida.

6. **(1)** The poet wants to escape from the big city to a smaller place "more suitable to the heart" (line 7).
7. **(1)** The tone is serious. The poet may be youthful, but that doesn't mean that the mood of the poem is. This poem is a serious expression of the poet's feelings about his voice (his identity).
8. **(2)** Every line except the last compares the poet's voice to an aspect of geography, but without the use of *like, as,* or *than.*
9. **(1)** The poet is using his voice as a symbol of how different he feels when he is away at school and when he is home in the land he loves.
10. **(3)** He is happiest when he is at home during summer months, when school is out and he can truly be himself.
11. **(1)** They are both similes, making comparisons using the word *like.*
12. **(4)** The second stanza names the places about which the poet's mother and grandmother sing.
13. **(3)** "Daughter" is the young girl's (poet's) mother. The mother and daughter in the poem are the poet's grandmother and mother.
14. **(3)** Line 9 says that the poet loves to hear the song sung.

CHAPTER 7
DRAMA

EXERCISE 1
Pages 146–147

1. **(1)** "Bunt? Two runs behind, bases loaded and they send Hodges up to bunt!"(lines 1–2) obviously refers to a baseball game that Richard is listening to or watching at home.
2. **(2)** To "stay on the wagon" is most likely a health measure since it is mentioned along with two other health measures: not smoking and proper diet. Richard also refers to being on the wagon when he drinks the soda.
3. **(3)** The stage directions tell you that Richard has settled back in the chaise where "he sits, smiling, remembering the scene" of the conversation.
4. **(3)** Richard complains that he has had "one continuous upset stomach" since he quit drinking (lines 30–31).
5. **(3)** In his memory sequence (lines 33–34), Richard recalls that Helen said she would call at ten o'clock.

EXERCISE 2
Page 149

1. **(2)** There are several clues in the passage. Cindy's father, the preacher, is gone, and her mother is now married to David.
2. **(2)** Molly feels that she and Cindy owe a debt of gratitude to David. She does not want to hear Cindy criticize the man who saved them from losing everything.
3. **(2)** David needs Cindy to attract more busines to the bar, especially on Friday nights, when her "pretty little face gets a lot of guys to buy a lot of drinks" (lines 5–6). He flatters her in an attempt to get what he wants.
4. **(1)** David had previously agreed that Cindy could have Friday nights off to attend her prayer meetings.

PRE-GED PRACTICE
EXERCISE 3
Pages 150–153

1. **(4)** Mel is in a state of mental anguish. In the opening lines, he says that he is not through with life and that he still has value and worth. Later, he alludes to being "halfway" to insanity (lines 48–49). In the final two lines, he expresses a desperate need for breathing space.
2. **(2)** Edna says that Mel lives like a "caged animal" (lines 5–6). Mel himself says he needs "just a little breathing space" (lines 59–60), and he knows that travel is not the answer.
3. **(1)** Edna's words show how frustrated she is. She says: "I am not the one who's doing this to you" (lines 52–53); "Don't talk to me like I'm insane" (lines 46–47); Then "what do you want from me?" (lines 55–56); and "What do you want from anyone?" (lines 56–57).
4. **(1)** This scene is all about Mel's desire to escape. Edna describes him as living like "a caged animal in a Second Avenue zoo." Mel is obviously the main character in a play that takes its name from his predicament (problem).
5. **(5)** The dialogue tells us that Davies' dreaming, groaning, and jabbering woke Aston up (lines 36–37).
6. **(4)** You can determine the meaning from the context. The word *groans* (line 25) provides the best clue. *Jabbering* refers to gibberish, or unintelligible talk.
7. **(1)** Davies takes pains to deny that he dreamed, jabbered, or was unaccustomed to sleeping in a bed.
8. **(1)** Aston asks Davies if he slept well and then gets the toaster, so you can infer that their conversation takes place in the morning.
9. **(1)** Aston is referring to himself in lines 32–34 when he says, "You got hold of the wrong bloke, mate."
10. **(2)** The phrase "dead out" refers to sleeping well (line 2).

CHAPTER 8
COMMENTARIES ON THE ARTS

EXERCISE 1
Pages 159–160

Part A

1. **(1)** F
   (2) O
   (3) F
2. **(1)** O
   (2) F
   (3) F
3. **(1)** F
   (2) F
   (3) O
4. **(1)** F
   (2) O
   (3) F

Part B

1. 3
2. 1
3. 4
4. 1

EXERCISE 2
Page 161

You should have listed the following words or phrases: (1) *strikes out*, (2) *simpy*, (3) *bad timing*, (4) *cardboard characters*, and (5) *witless plots.*

EXERCISE 3
Page 162

Your answer should have included the following: (1) *remarkable*, (2) *richly imagined*, (3) *daring*, (4) *bold*, (5) *ruthlessly comical*, (6) *intellectually stimulating*, (7) *finest*, and (8) *effective.*

EXERCISE 4
Page 163

1. *smart, spunky*
2. *heart-pounding*
3. "I wouldn't be surprised if she is nominated for a raft of honors."
4. "superior thriller," "brilliant performances"

EXERCISE 5
Page 164

1. (d), (f), (e)
2. (a), (c), (g)
3. (b), (h)

PRE-GED PRACTICE
EXERCISE 6
Pages 165–167

1. **(3)** Benny recounts several unuseful pieces of advice his friends gave him once they learned he was going to do television.
2. **(3)** Benny praises the competence of the technicians who "face the problems that are constantly cropping up with speed, skill, and imagination."
3. **(5)** In the last sentence of the article, Benny notes that "the movie industry would do well, even at this early stage, to adapt many of the steamlined methods of television."
4. **(2)** The entire passage is lighthearted (humorous) but informative as well.
5. **(2)** In this sentence Benny is saying that it would take Hollywood weeks to duplicate, or copy, the stage scenes that television directors set up each day.
6. **(4)** In this sentence Benny is discussing the phenomenal, or remarkable, progress which the television industry had already made.
7. **(3)** This is a very funny line—a good example of Benny's ability to create a comedic expression.

EXERCISE 7
Pages 168–169

1. In the first paragraph, it mentions that he visited the 8055 in Korea.
2. The 8055 was a mobile army surgical hospital during the Korean War.
3. The third sentence says that, after the war, the 8055 became a permanent facility.
4. The fourth sentence mentions their taped conversations with nurses, doctors, and chopper pilots.
5. Larry Gelbart says, "We got a taste of the real thing, and it was very hard to come back and be funny after that."
6. The whole point of the passage was the great improvement in the third year. This implies that during the first two years, the show was still growing toward its best work.
7. The letters stand for *mobile army surgical hospital.* This information is given in the bracketed portion of the third sentence.
8. Reynolds was the producer of the show.
9. Four reasons include being finally secure, having better ratings, having less trouble with censors, and being able to do much more of what they wanted to do on the show.

EXERCISE 8
Pages 170–171

1. **(1)** Paul Robeson's acting career is the theme that unites all the details in the passage.
2. **(2)** Robeson starred in *The Emperor Jones*. He became closely identified with the role of Brutus Jones. You can infer from these two facts that Brutus Jones was the title character in the London play.
3. **(2)** His role as Othello is mentioned in the fifth sentence of the final paragraph.
4. 4, 2, 5, 3, 1
5. Your answer should include any five of the following: *expressive features, resonant voice, tremendous sensitivity, dignity, simplicity, true passion, very experienced, mature, dignified, unforgettable, a high point in the history of American theater.*

EXERCISE 9
Pages 172–173

Part A

1. (d)	4. (a)
2. (f)	5. (c)
3. (b)	6. (e)

Part B

1. The setting is stated in the second sentence. It is a traveling theater in the form of a huge boat on the Mississippi River.
2. **(4)** The high price of the newest production is mentioned, but not in a critical way. The other choices are specifically mentioned as flaws in earlier productions.
3. **(4)** This is a rave review filled with positive statements about Prince's 1994 production.
4. Positive phrases include: "spectacular stagecraft"; "wonderfully imaginative"; "lavishly constructed"; and "near perfect staging."

EXERCISE 10
Pages 174–175

1. Van Gogh was in the town of Arles, in southern France. This is stated in the first sentence.
2. Van Gogh. The second paragraph mentions his letters to his family.
3. Your answer should include two of the following: "nearly half-dead"; "I have just slept sixteen hours at a stretch"; "I am all right again"; "my eyes are still tired." See paragraphs 3 and 4.
4. Complete or absolute restfulness. This is stated in the last sentence.
5. Answers will vary.
6. new uses of color, different styles and subjects
7. white
8. illness and long hours spent painting

EXERCISE 11
Page 176

1. Berlin, Germany. See the first and last sentences of the first paragraph.
2. She photographed poets, singers, actors, dancers, and people she admired. This information is given in the first paragraph.
3. By photographing artists and other creative people, she was producing a record of creativity in the arts during that 100-year period.
4. Your answer should include four of the following: herself, Robert Frost, May Sarton, Edward Steichen, Albert Einstein.
5. Her self-portrait "most clearly shows her passion for the art form that occupied her attention for over sixty years. She appears to be rushing into the picture frame, her hair flying a bit and her eyes alight."

PRE-GED PRACTICE
EXERCISE 12
Pages 177–178

1. **(2)** "Poetry is like the bird's song" is the only simile among the choices because it uses the word *like* to compare two things.
2. **(1)** That the best poems have music and magic in common is stated in the last sentence of the second paragraph.
3. **(5)** The main idea of the passage is the joyful experience that reading poetry should be. This idea is stated in the first sentence.
4. **(4)** The fact that the delight of poetry will be lost can be inferred from the first paragraph.

EXERCISE 13
Pages 178–179

1. a small town in Ohio
2. middle-age romance
3. This is not a book that is funny or worth reading.
4. Possible answers: "the publishers should have had second thoughts"; "an unlikely story about two uninteresting characters"; "drawn-out bad puns"; "worn-out jokes"; "they aren't even as substantial as the floppy disks they were no doubt stored on"; "a snooze in Dullsville"; "cardboard characters . . . paper-thin."
5. Possible answer: The name of the critic is not given, so the person's reputation as a credible reviewer is not known.

PRE-GED PRACTICE
EXERCISE 14
Pages 180–183

1. **(4)** The first and second paragraphs specify the subject of the exhibit: various kinds of work by Latino artists.
2. **(2)** Castillo's studio includes his own sculpture, and the exhibit includes contemporary art. These facts alone make it false to say that the studio is devoted to ancient art.
3. **(4)** The rough and powerful retablos are described in the last sentence.
4. **(1)** Bou and Uribe are described as contemporary painters in the second sentence of the next to last paragraph.
5. **(1)** This is a very favorable review.
6. **(2)** The passage makes no mention of Honduras.
7. **(1)** You can infer from context clues that *riveting* means "exciting to read."
8. **(2)** That the information was received from the *Apollo* astronauts is stated in the third sentence.
9. **(4)** This statement is a personal judgment. All the other statements are facts that can be proved.
10. **(1)** This is what the reviewer means when he says that the writer "brings the astronauts to life."
11. **(2)** Hanging from a cliff implies great danger; so does the in-flight explosion of an oxygen tank.
12. **(5)** You can tell from the first paragraph that the reviewer has the highest possible opinion of this film. The top rating is four stars.
13. **(5)** All of the choices are mentioned in the second paragraph.
14. **(5)** The first sentence of the second paragraph names the main subjects of this documentary: William Gates and Arthur Agee.
15. **(1)** When a reviewer says that a particular film "is what the movies are for," you can conclude that he is recommending it for all audiences.
16. **(3)** The long commute and the change to a largely white school imply that William and Arthur face difficulties ahead.

ANSWER KEY

Glossary

action: the sequence of events in a drama—comparable to the plot of a novel

analyze: to break something down into its parts to understand the whole, as in a passage, paragraph, or graphic

application of ideas: taking information from one source and applying it to another situation

atmosphere: the mood or general feeling in which a story is rooted

B

bias: a writer's personal opinions that give the writing a positive or negative slant

C

character: a fictional person in a work of literature

characterization: the writer's presentation of a character through description, action, dialogue, thoughts, and feelings

classify: to put information into categories that enhance understanding

climax: the turning point in the action of a play or the plot of a novel

comedy: a drama that takes a light approach to its subject; characterized by funny or satirical dialogue and a happy ending

commentary: a review or essay about popular culture

comparison: the presentation of similarities between people, things, or ideas

conflict: the struggle between opposing forces in a story, such as a person against others, himself or herself, society, or nature

context: the surrounding words or sentences that help explain the meaning of a particular word or expression

contrast: the presentation of differences between people, things, or ideas

critical essay: a subjective and sophisticated type of commentary on the arts

D

descriptive language: writing characterized by vivid, colorful words and phrases

dialect: a regional variation of standard speech

dialogue: the words spoken by the characters in a drama

drama: a story, written in the form of a dialogue, to be performed onstage

drawing a conclusion: making an interpretation based on facts or supporting details

E

editorial: a column in a newspaper or magazine expressing the opinion of the publication's editor

effects: things that happened as the result of an action or an event

ellipsis points: punctuation consisting of three dots in a row, used to indicate that someone's voice has trailed off or that words in a sentence have been omitted

essay: an informative article about a book, play, or specific topic

F

fact: a true statement that can be proved through research

fiction: novels, short stories, and other literature that deals with imaginary characters and events

figurative language: words chosen for effect, not literal truth, to express a speaker's message

first-person point of view: a type of writing in which the author is also the narrator or main character in the story

G

Great Depression: a worldwide business slump when the U.S. stock market crashed in the 1930s

I

idea: in drama, the underlying message of a play

imagery: the mental pictures suggested by descriptive language in prose or poetry

inference: an educated guess about something that is not directly stated in a passage but is strongly hinted at or implied

informative essay: a commentary on the arts written for the general reader and designed to inform without judging

irony: a type of humor that implies a difference between what is true and what should be true

L

literal language: words that mean exactly what is stated, with no other meaning implied

M

main idea: a statement that tells what a whole selection is about

metaphor: a comparison made without the use of the word *like, as,* or *than*

motivation: in drama, the factors that reveal the reasons for a character's behavior

N

nonfiction prose: reading selections that present factual information or that express a viewpoint

O

opinion: a personal judgment or belief

order of importance: organizing information in a paragraph or passage upward from a small detail to the central idea, or downward from the most important point

P

personification: giving the qualities of a living thing to something that is not alive, or giving human qualities to something that is not human

pitch: the musical quality of a voice

place: the physical setting in which a story occurs

plot: in fiction, the sequence of events leading to the climax and then the conclusion

poetry: writing in verse form designed to appeal to the senses and the imagination; characterized by figurative language, rhythm, and rhyme

point of view: how a particular event or series of events look to a specific individual

propaganda: deceptive writing intended to influence readers by misrepresenting the truth

prose fiction: type of writing that includes novels and short stories and deals with imaginary characters and events

R

reference: a source of objective information, such as an encyclopedia, a telephone directory, an almanac, or a road map

resolution: ending part of a story

response: in drama, the reaction of a character to a situation, event, or remark

review: a personal critique of a movie, book, play, or television or radio program

rhyme: the repetition of sounds

rhythm: the beat or pattern of language or sound

S

sarcasm: a tone of bitter humor, usually directed at a specific target.

scan: read quickly but closely to find a specific fact or detail

sequence: the order in which things are presented or arranged

setting: the combination of place or location, time, and atmosphere; the background against which a story takes place

simile: a comparison that uses the word *like, as,* or *than*

social drama: a type of drama dealing with familiar problems in true-to-life situations

soliloquy: dialogue spoken aloud by a single actor alone upon the stage

stage directions: in the text of a drama, written material apart from the dialogue that explains a character's thoughts, feelings, or physical movements

stanza: in a poem or song, a verse or several lines that stand together

style: the general category of a piece of writing (formal, persuasive, informative, etc.) based on the type of words and sentences used

subjective: characterized by opinion

supporting details: items of information that support the main idea of a passage

symbolism: having one thing represent something else, such as a heart representing love

T

theme: the implied message that underlies and gives meaning to a work of fiction or drama

time: when a story takes place—in the past, present, or future

tone: the emotional character of a piece of writing or, in drama, of a character's voice

tragedy: a drama in which a leading character comes to ruin as the result of a character flaw or overwhelming outside forces

V

volume: in drama, the loudness or softness of a character's voice

Index